TRUE SURVIVAL GRAPH

ANIMAL ATTACKS

by Jarred Luján

illustrated by Rudy Faber

CAPSTONE PRESS
a capstone imprint

Published by Capstone Press, an imprint of Capstone
1710 Roe Crest Drive, North Mankato, Minnesota 56003
capstonepub.com

Library of Congress Cataloging-in-Publication Data
Names: Luján, Jarred, author. | Faber, Rudy, illustrator.
Title: Animal attacks / by Jarred Luján ; illustrated by Rudy Faber.
Description: North Mankato, Minnesota : Capstone Press, [2024] | Series:
True survival graphics | Includes bibliographical references. | Audience:
Ages 9–11 | Audience: Grades 4–6 | Summary: "A grumpy grizzly bear attacks a
young hunter. A huge hippopotamus strikes an unsuspecting tourist. A ferocious
great white shark chomps into an experienced surfer. These shocking, true
animal attacks could have ended in tragedy—but they didn't! What happened
to the people who came face to face with these terrifying creatures? And how
did they survive to tell their tales? Young readers will find out in this
easy-to-read hi-lo graphic novel that will keep them on the edge
of their seats!"— Provided by publisher.
Identifiers: LCCN 2023014707 (print) | LCCN 2023014708 (ebook) |
ISBN 9781669058694 (hardcover) | ISBN 9781669058861 (paperback) |
ISBN 9781669058878 (pdf) | ISBN 9781669058892 (kindle edition) |
ISBN 9781669058885 (epub)
Subjects: LCSH: Animal attacks—Juvenile literature. | Animal attacks—Comic
books, strips, etc. | LCGFT: Graphic novels.
Classification: LCC QL100.5 .L85 2024 (print) | LCC QL100.5 (ebook) | DDC
591.5/3—dc23/eng/20230518
LC record available at https://lccn.loc.gov/2023014707
LC ebook record available at https://lccn.loc.gov/2023014708

Editorial Credits
Editor: Christopher Harbo; Designer: Tracy Davies;
Production Specialist: Katy LaVigne

All internet sites appearing in back matter were available and accurate when
this book was sent to press.

TABLE OF CONTENTS

INTRODUCTION

UNFRIENDLY NEIGHBORS!

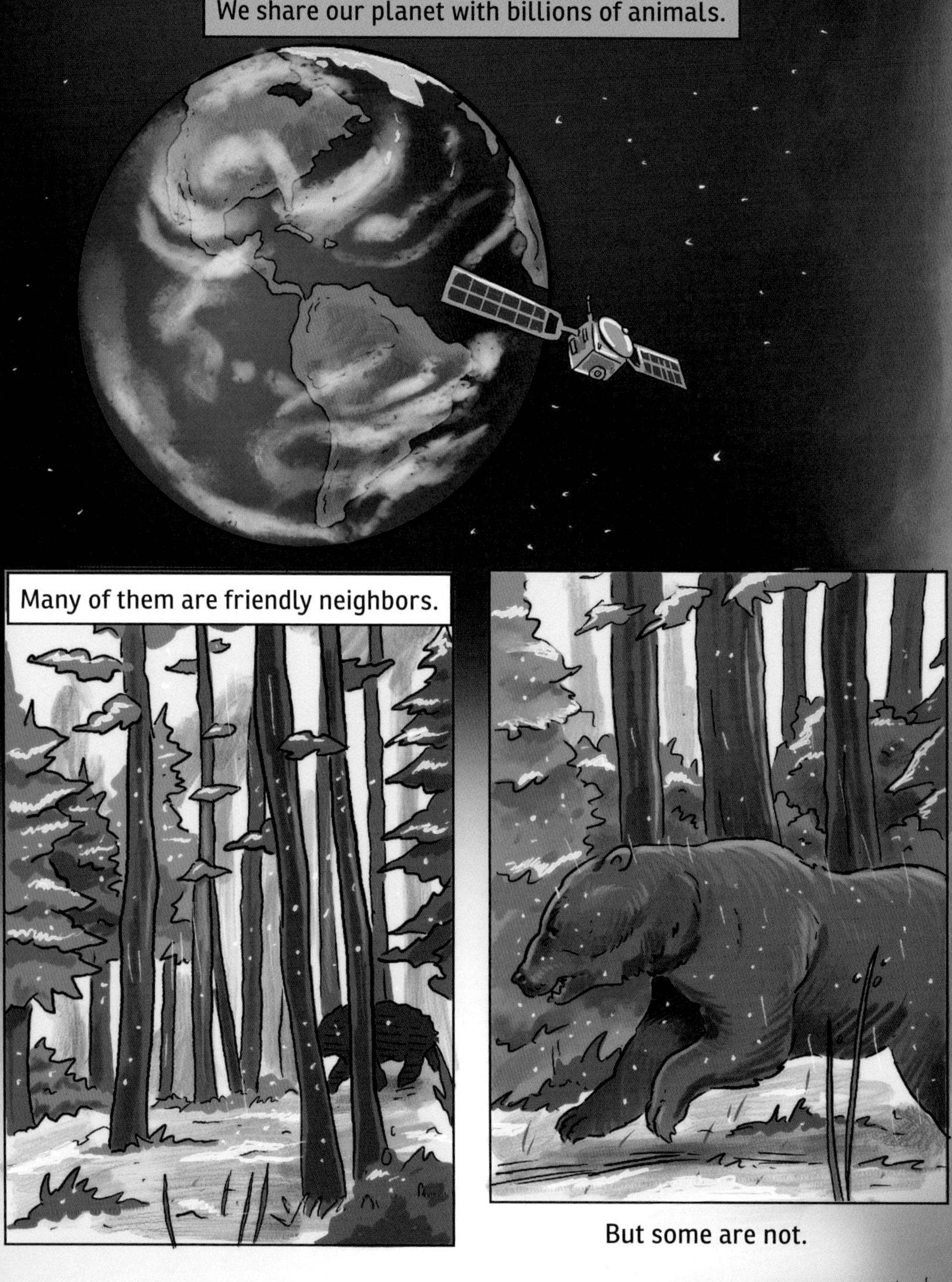
We share our planet with billions of animals.
Many of them are friendly neighbors.
But some are not.

In the stories that follow, regular people met a few of these unfriendly neighbors.

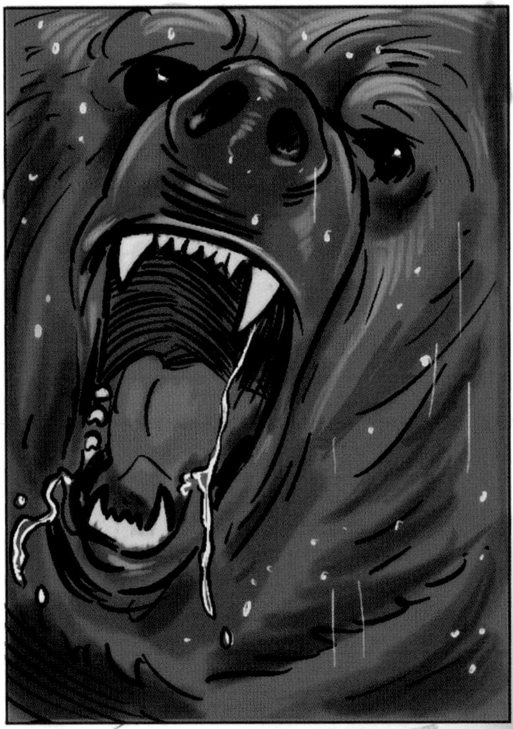

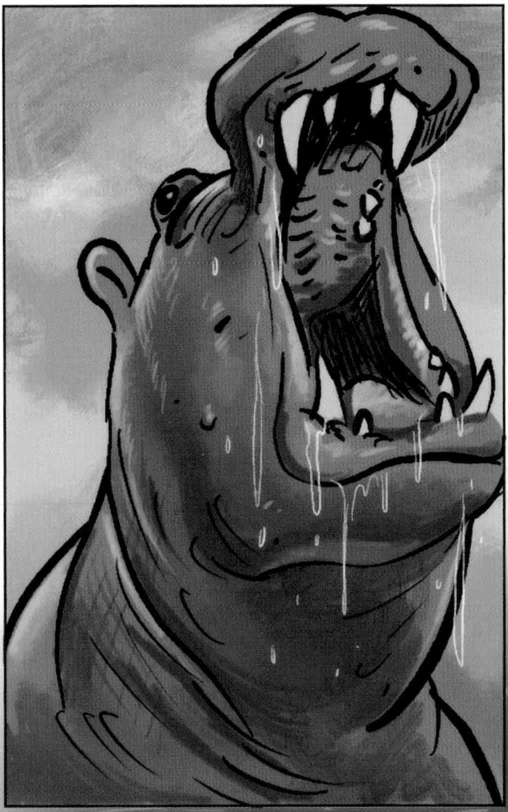

Find out how they lived to tell the tale!

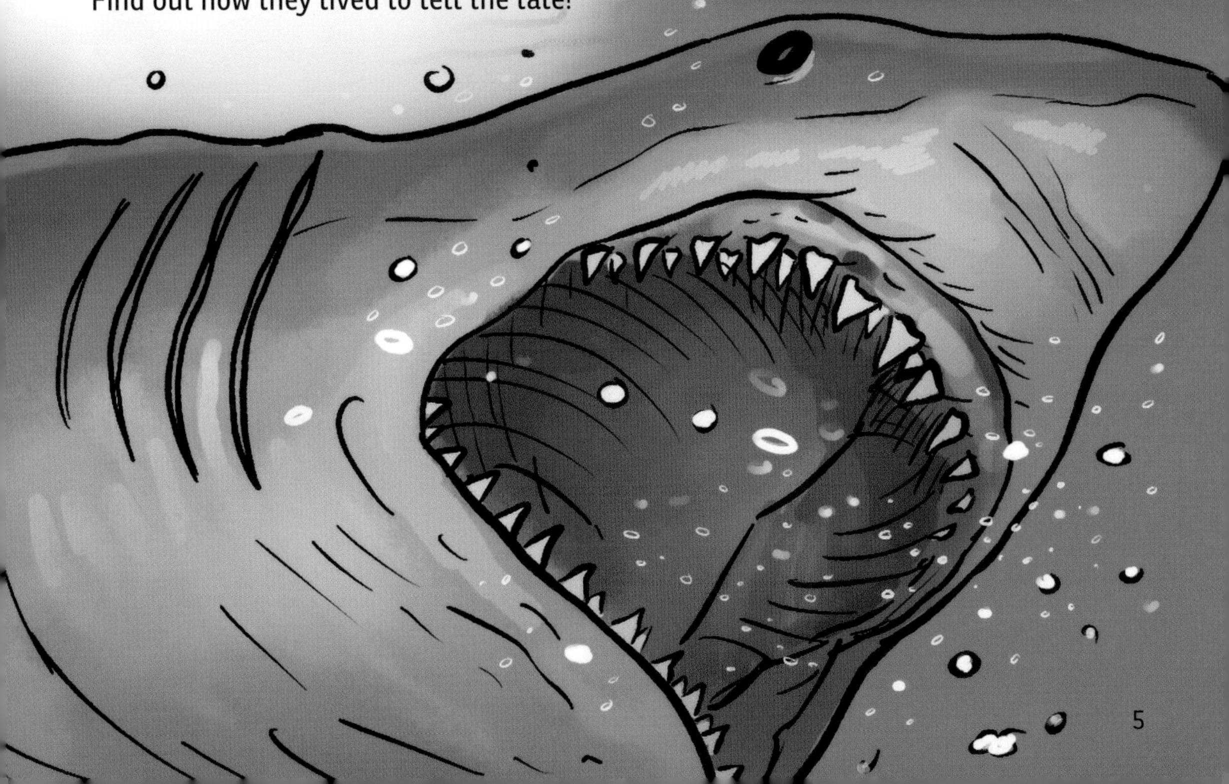

CHAPTER 1
A RUDE AWAKENING!

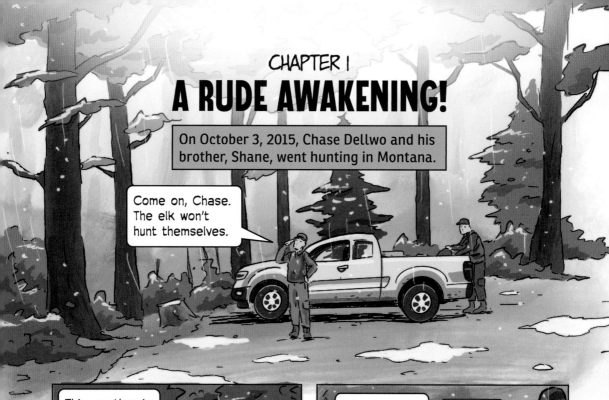

On October 3, 2015, Chase Dellwo and his brother, Shane, went hunting in Montana.

Come on, Chase. The elk won't hunt themselves.

This weather is terrible, Shane.

Some elk have moved through here.

That's for sure.

You walk the creek bed. Try to get them moving.

I'll head to that ridge and pick them off as they come up.

Yeah, I can do that.

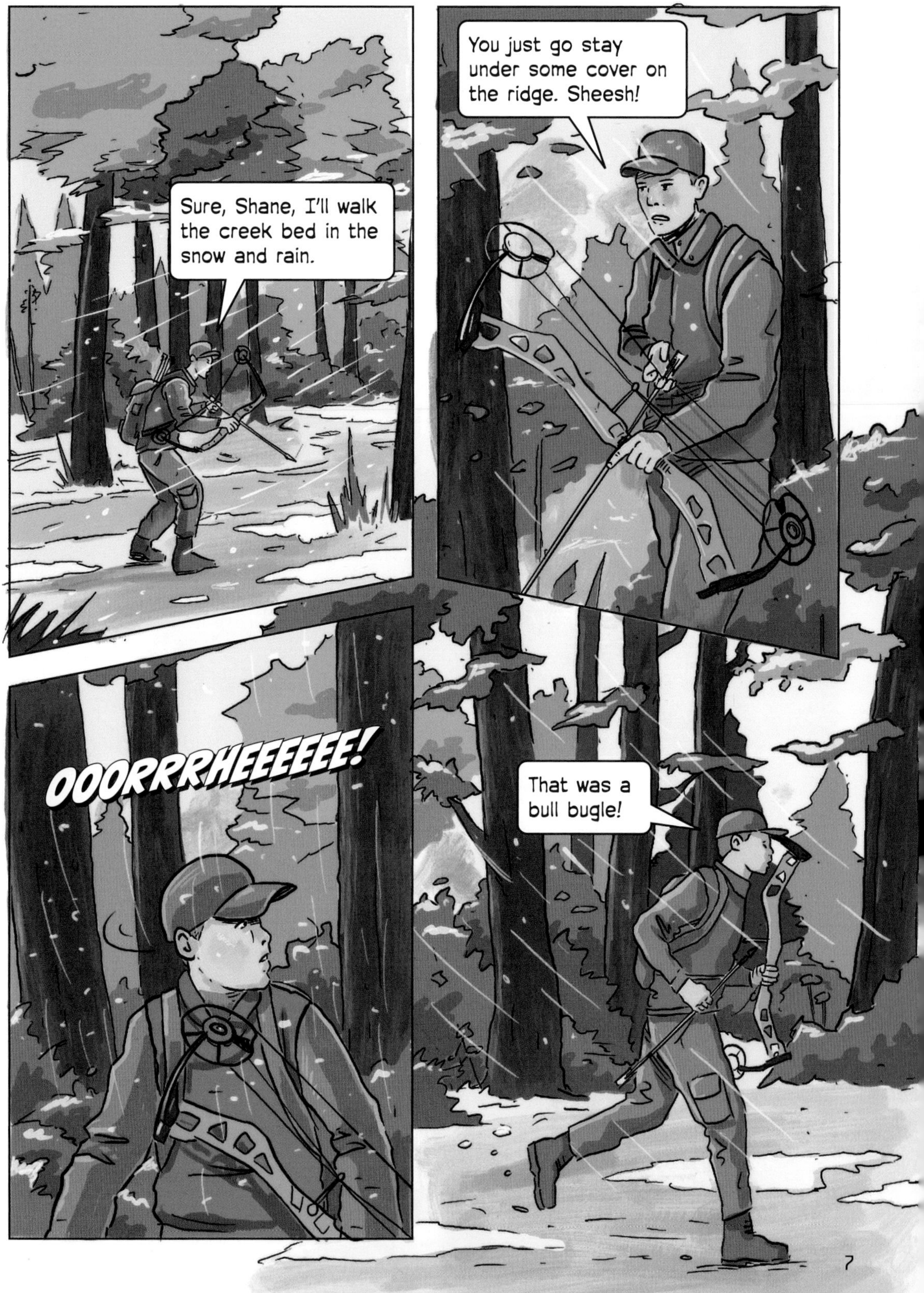
Sure, Shane, I'll walk the creek bed in the snow and rain.
You just go stay under some cover on the ridge. Sheesh!
OOORRRHEEEEEE!
That was a bull bugle!

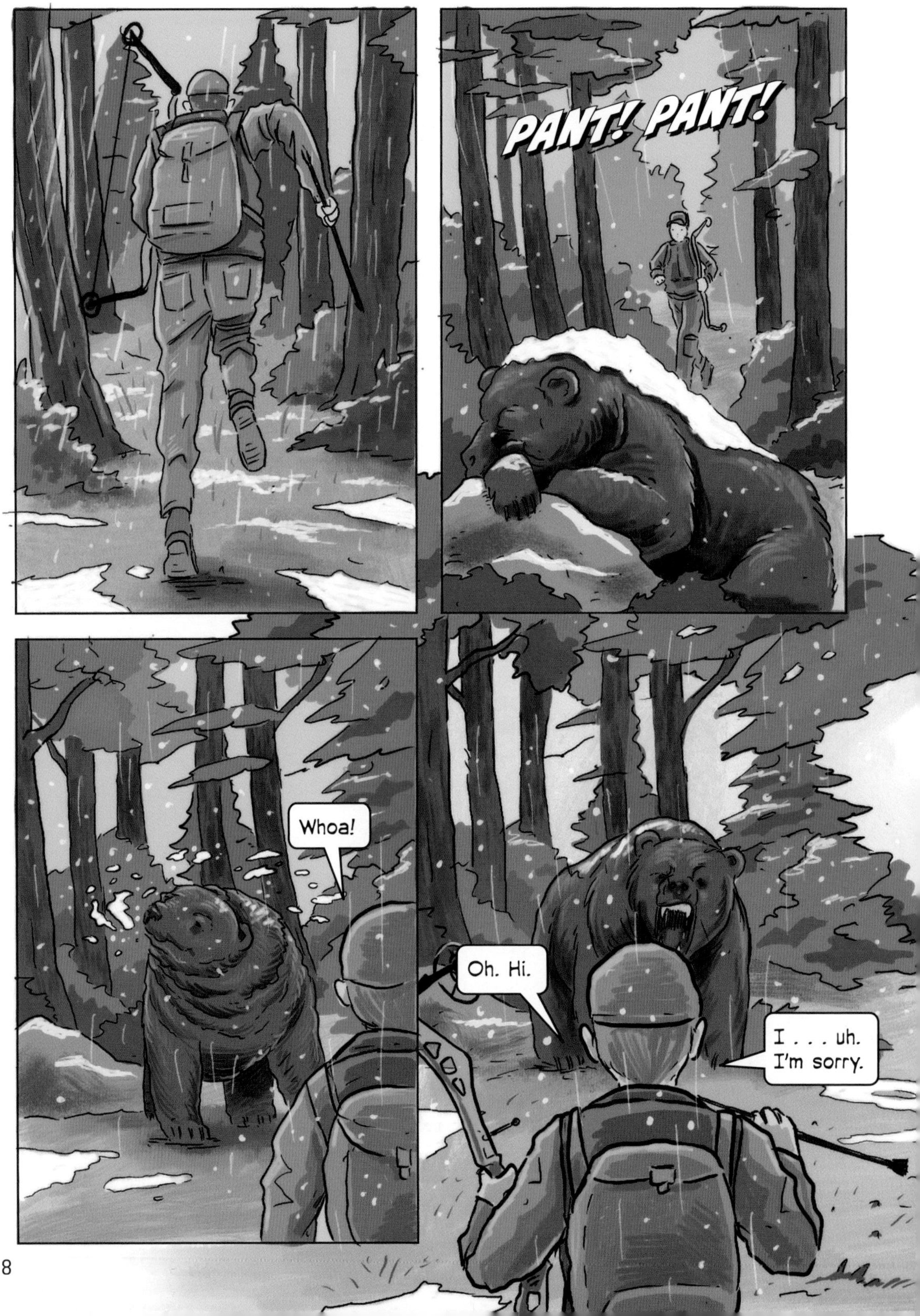
PANT! PANT!
Whoa!
Oh. Hi.
I . . . uh.
I'm sorry.

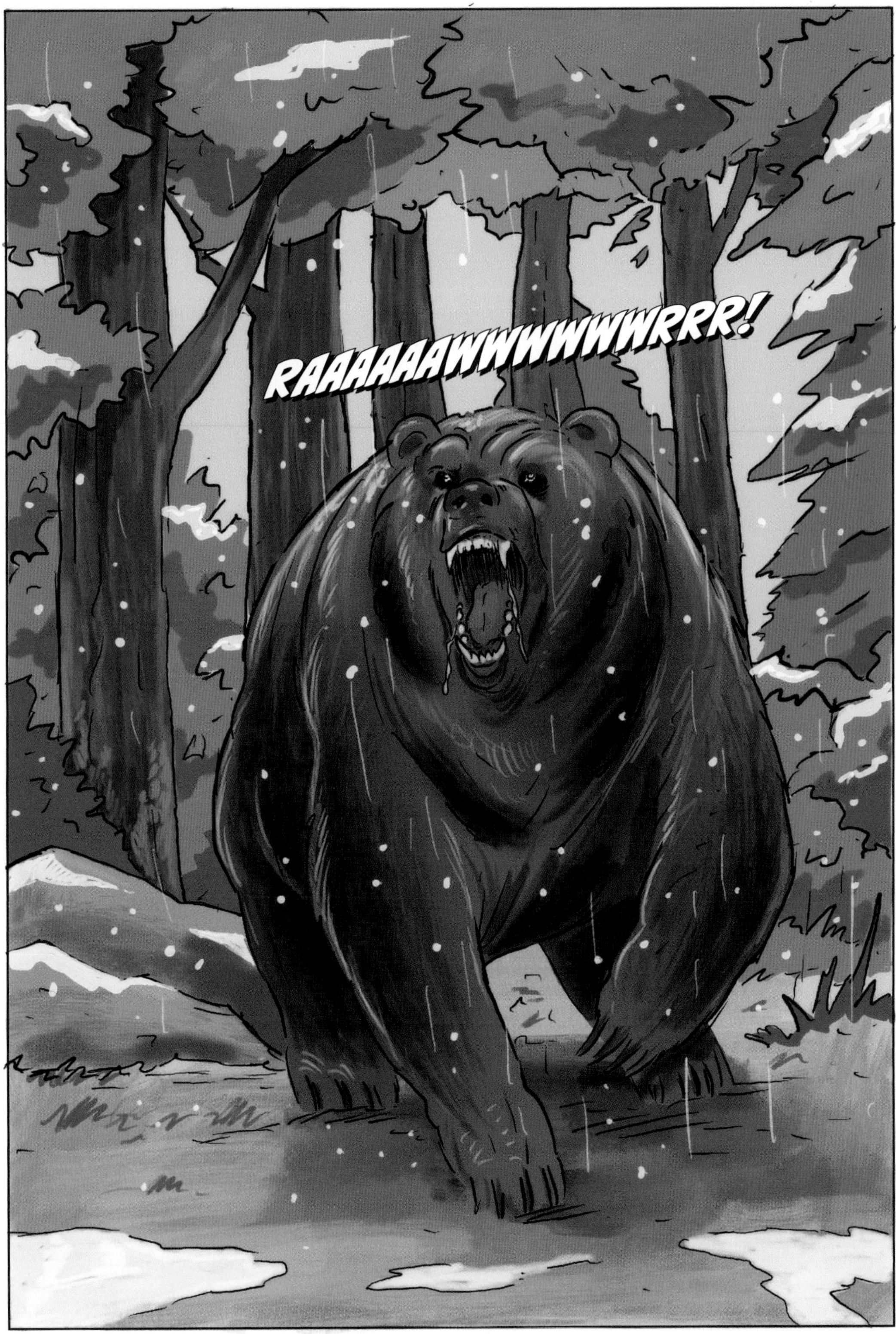
RAAAAAAWWWWWWRRR!

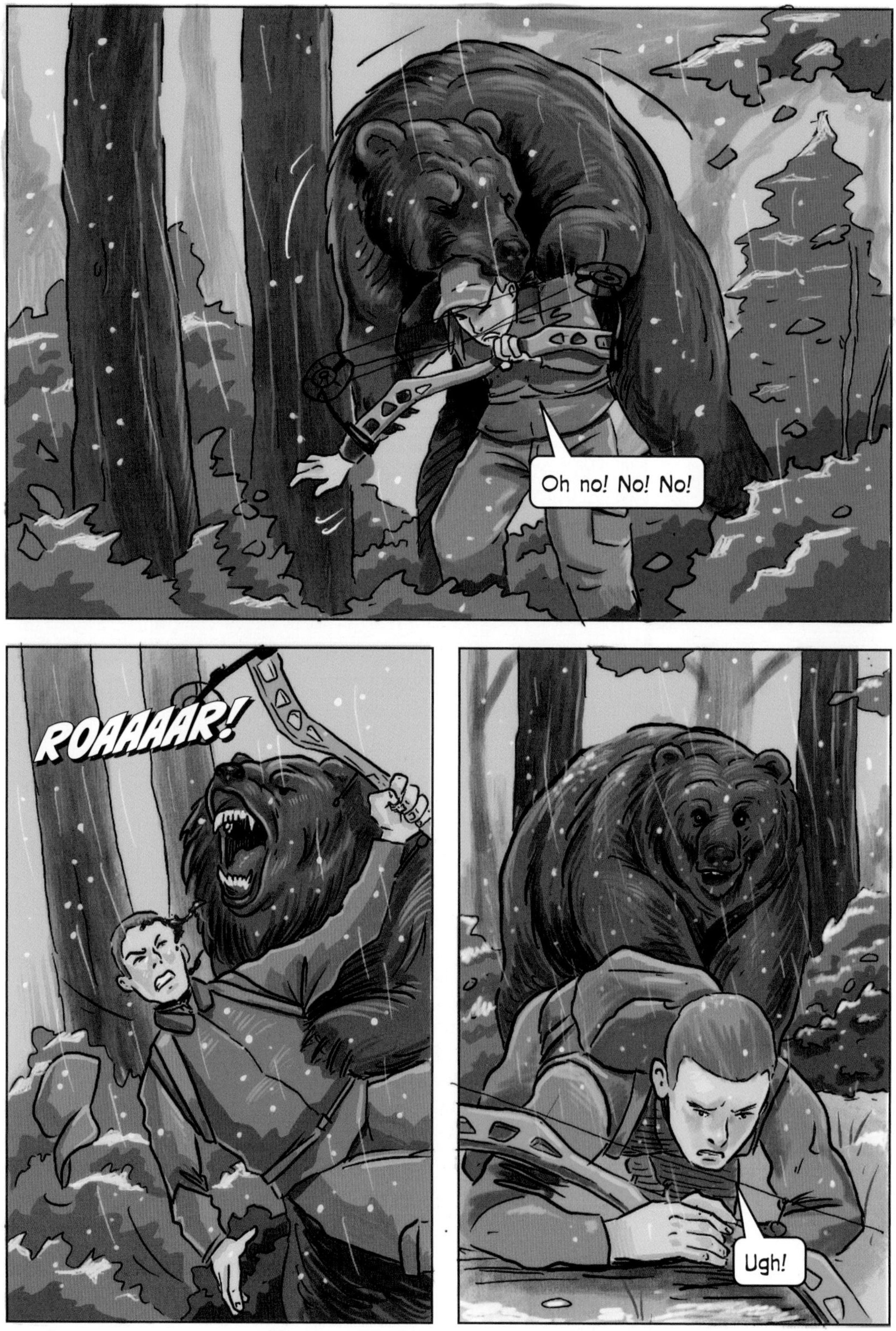
Oh no! No! No!
ROAAAAR!
Ugh!

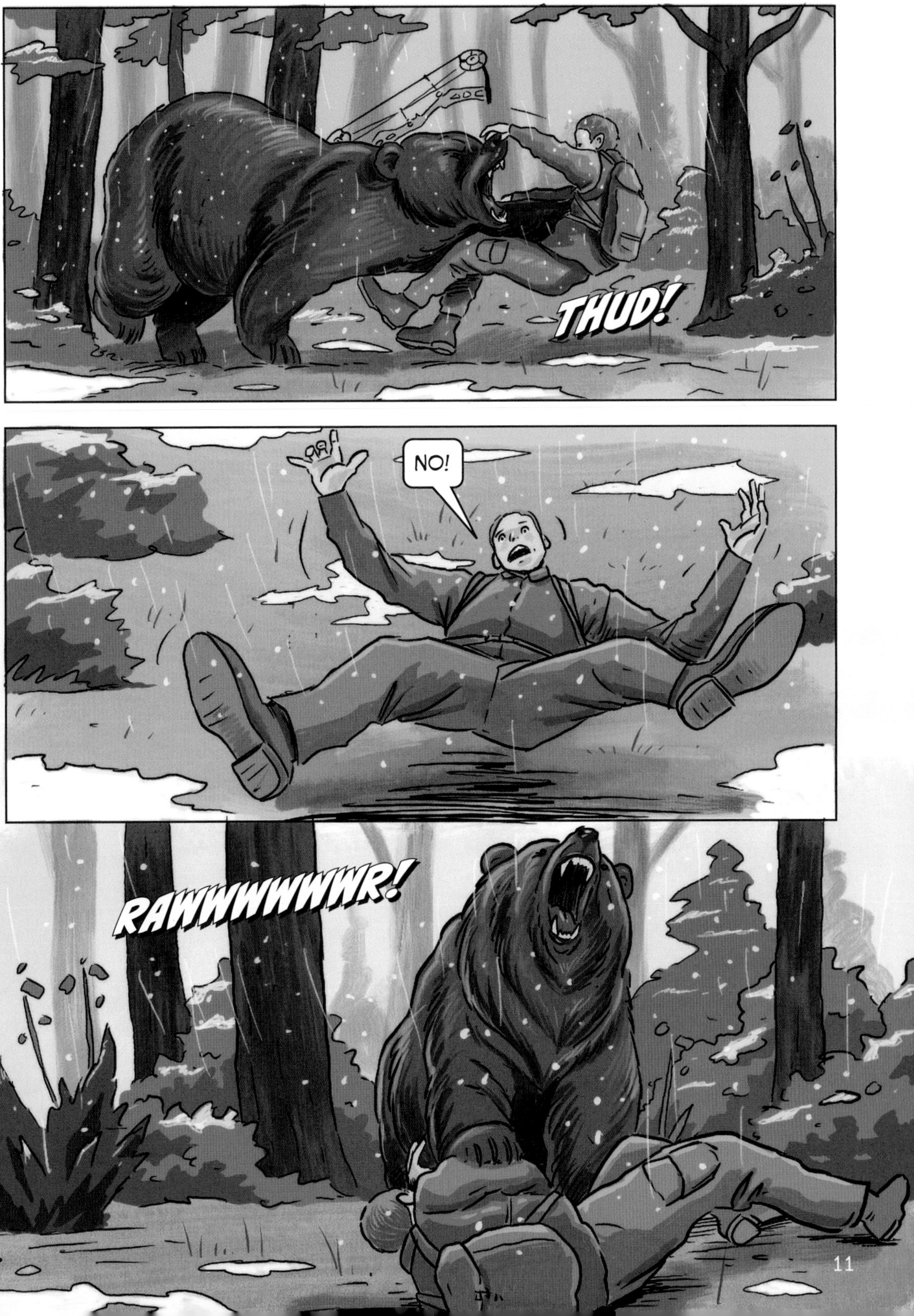
THUD!
NO!
RAWWWWWWR!

Now, things looked pretty grim for Chase.

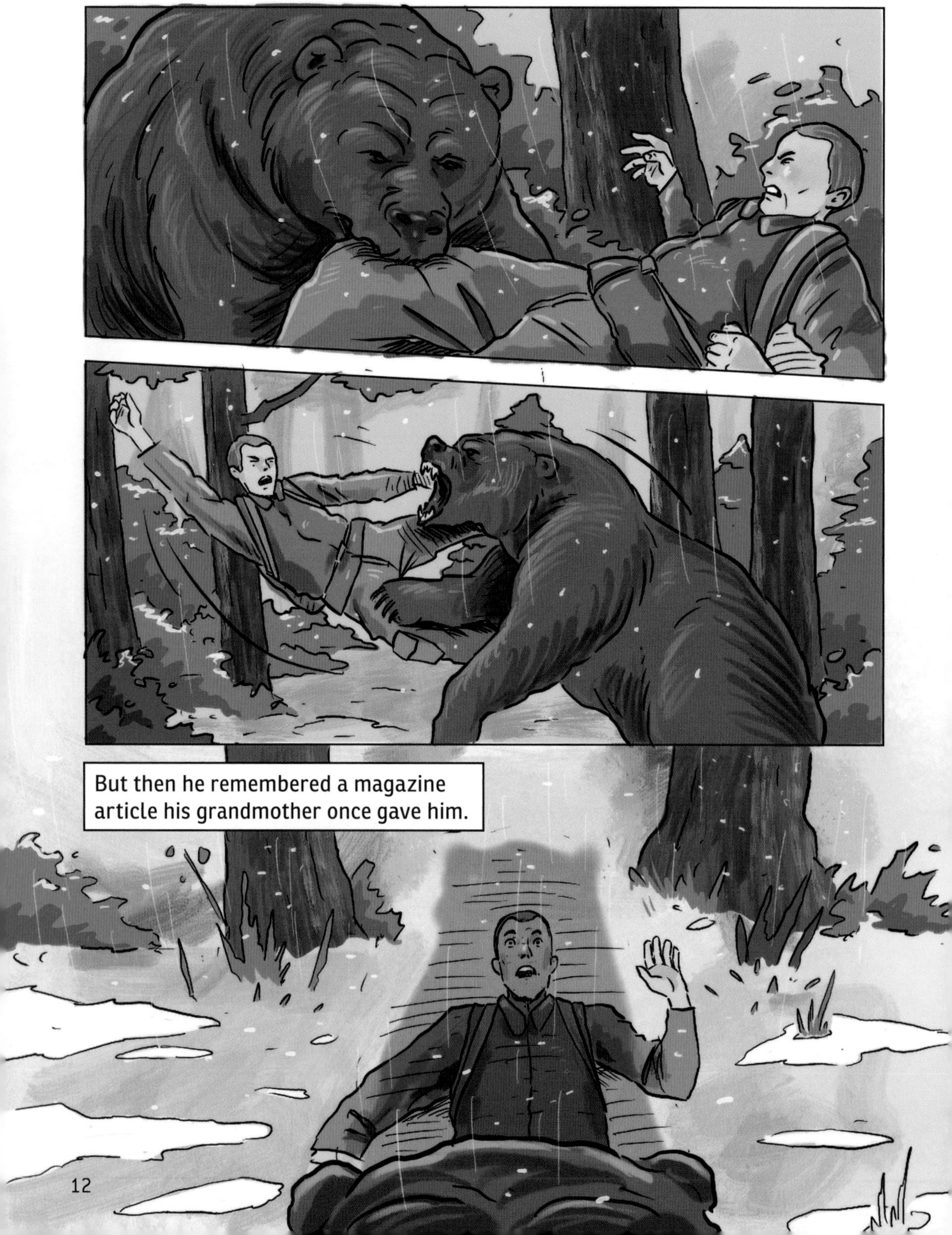
But then he remembered a magazine article his grandmother once gave him.

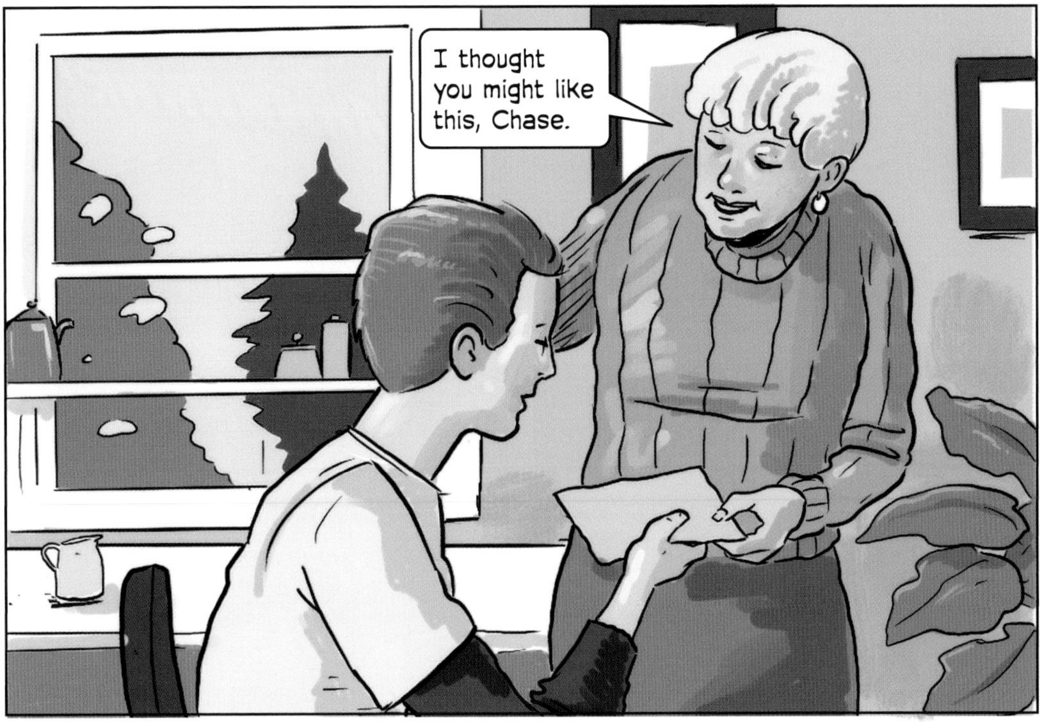
I thought you might like this, Chase.

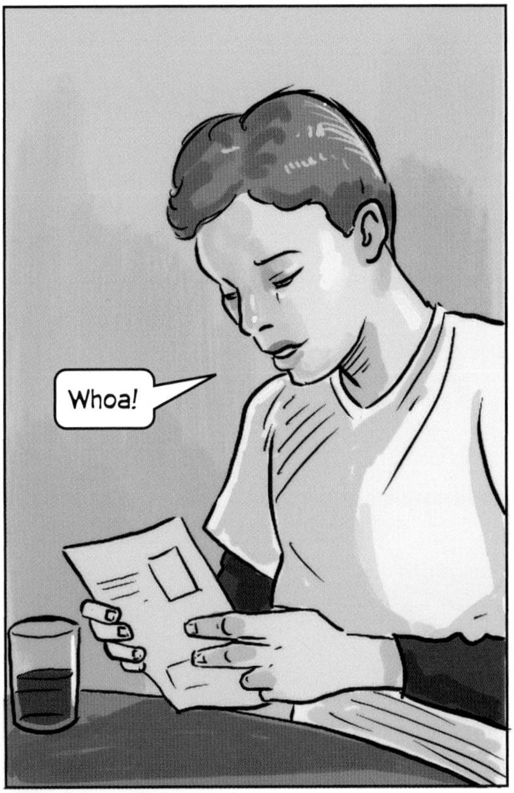
Whoa!

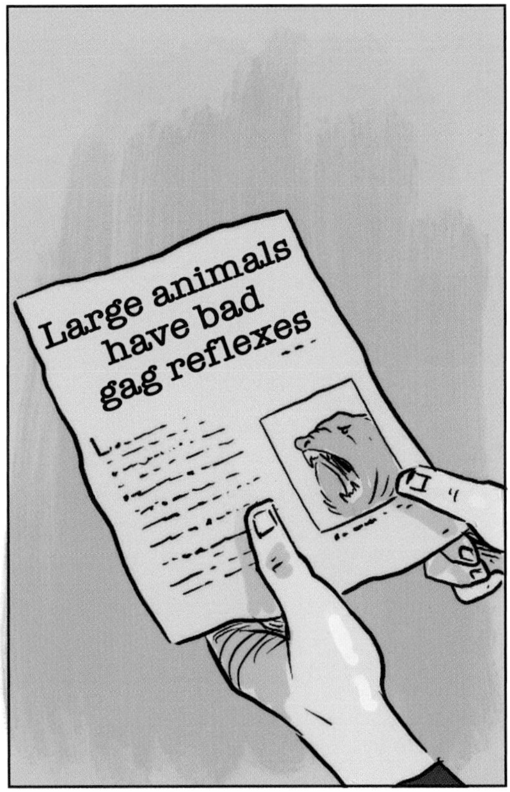
Large animals have bad gag reflexes

Bloodied and battered, Chase stood up to face the bear.

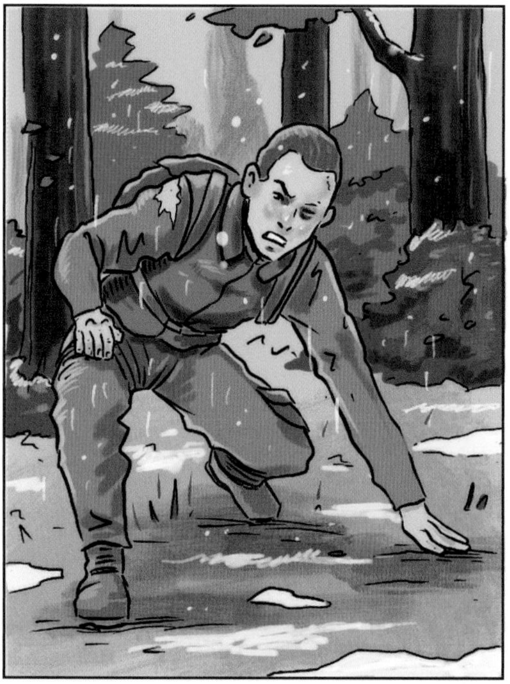

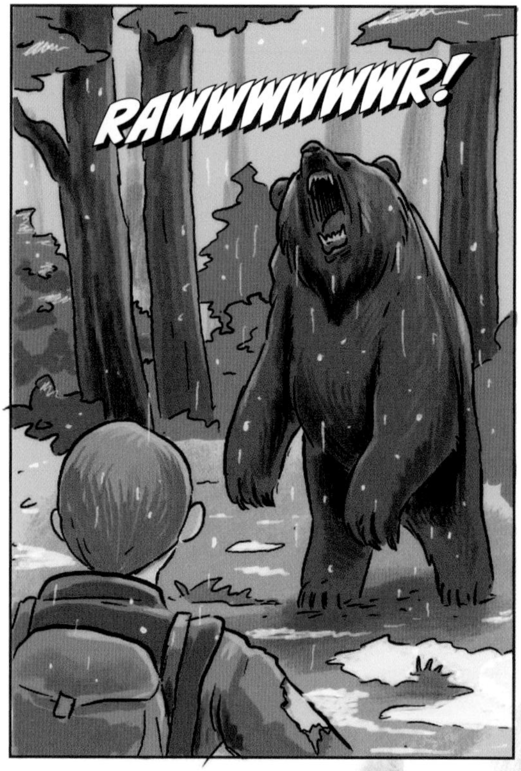
RAWWWWWWR!

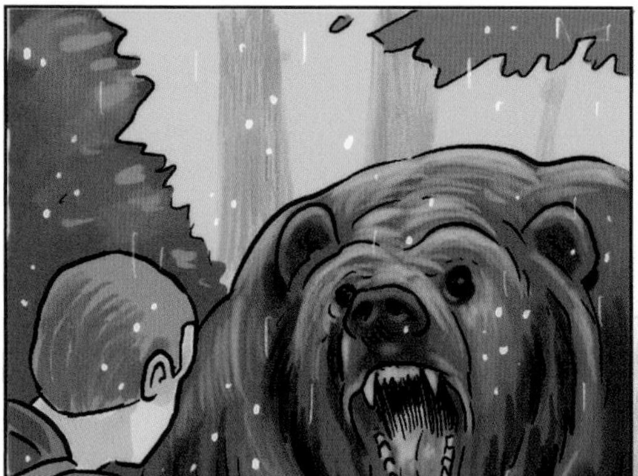

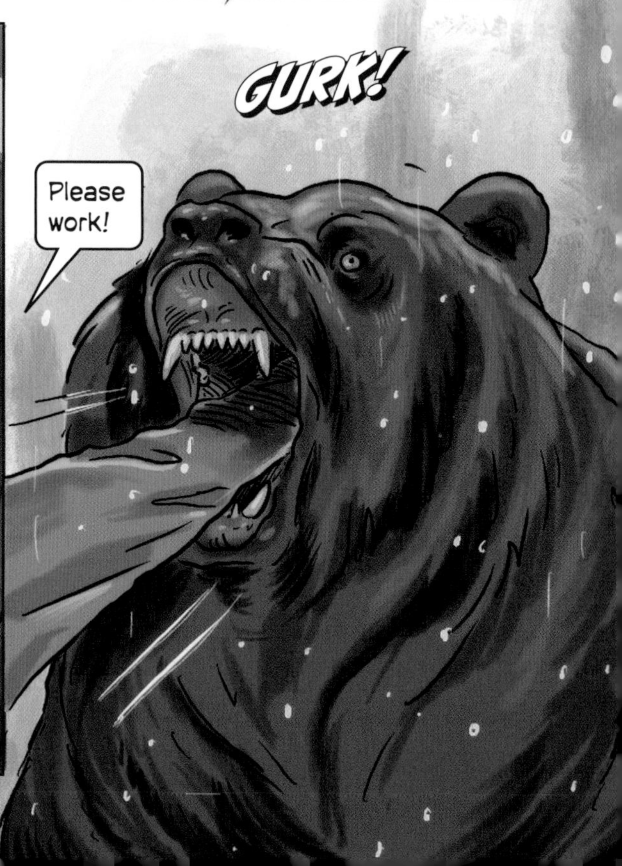
GURK!
Please work!

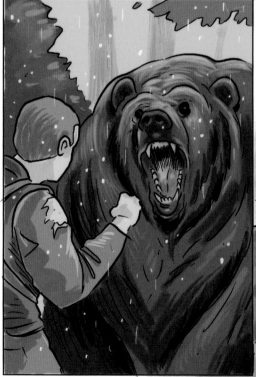

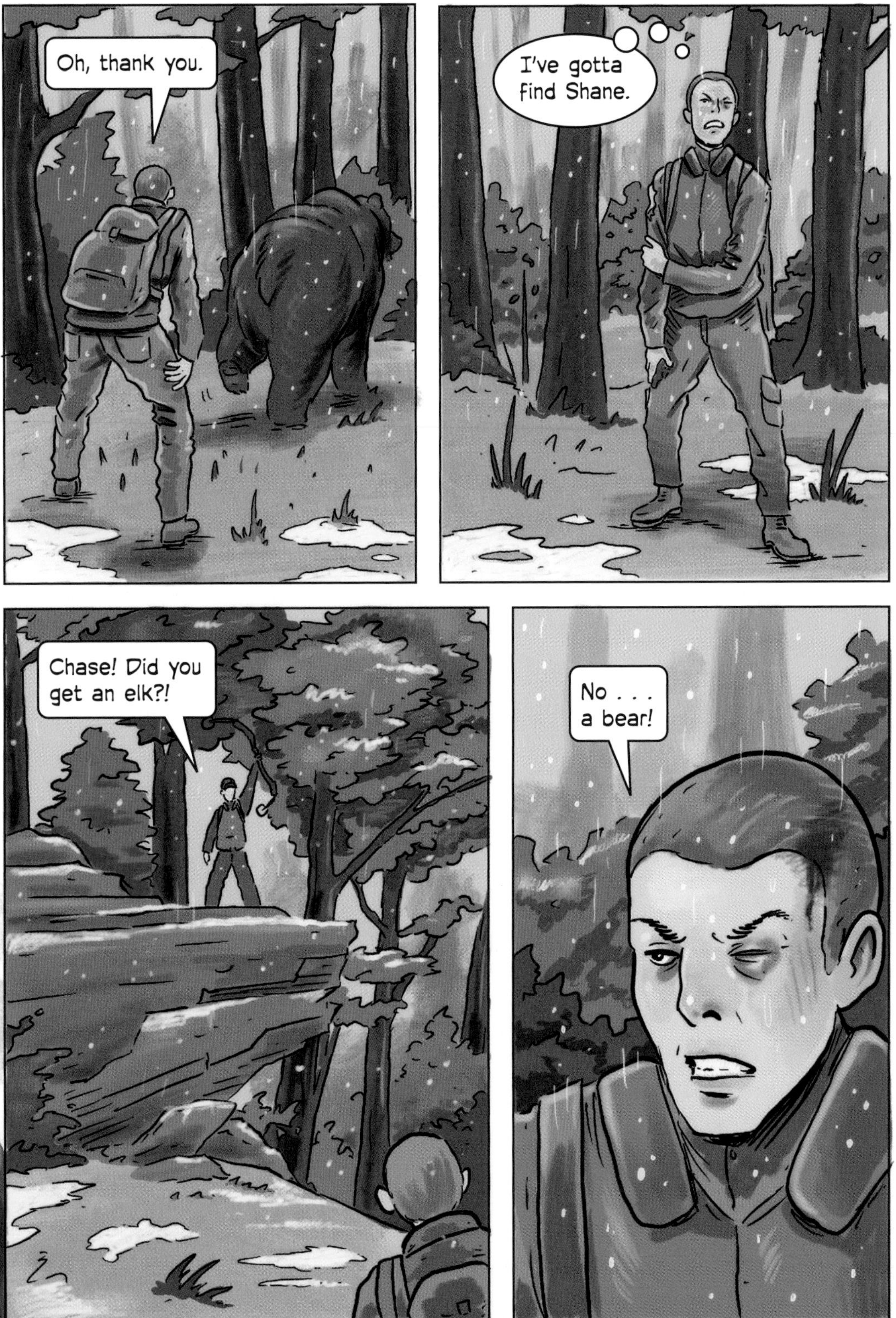
Oh, thank you.
I've gotta find Shane.
Chase! Did you get an elk?!
No . . . a bear!

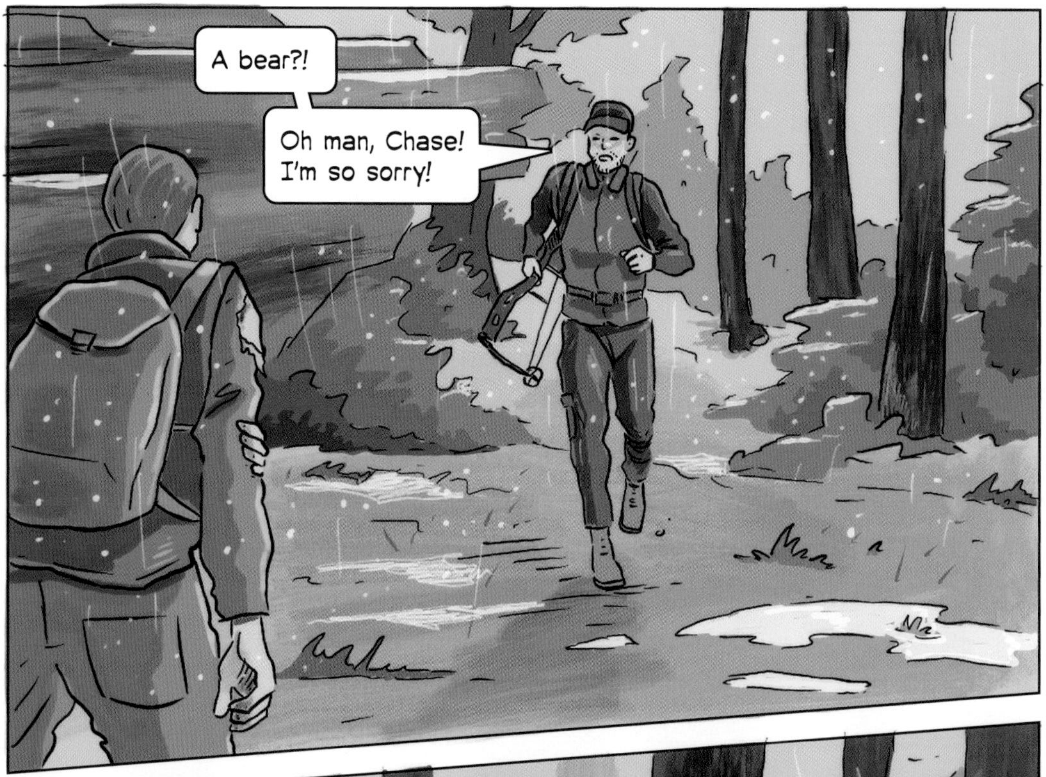
A bear?!
Oh man, Chase! I'm so sorry!

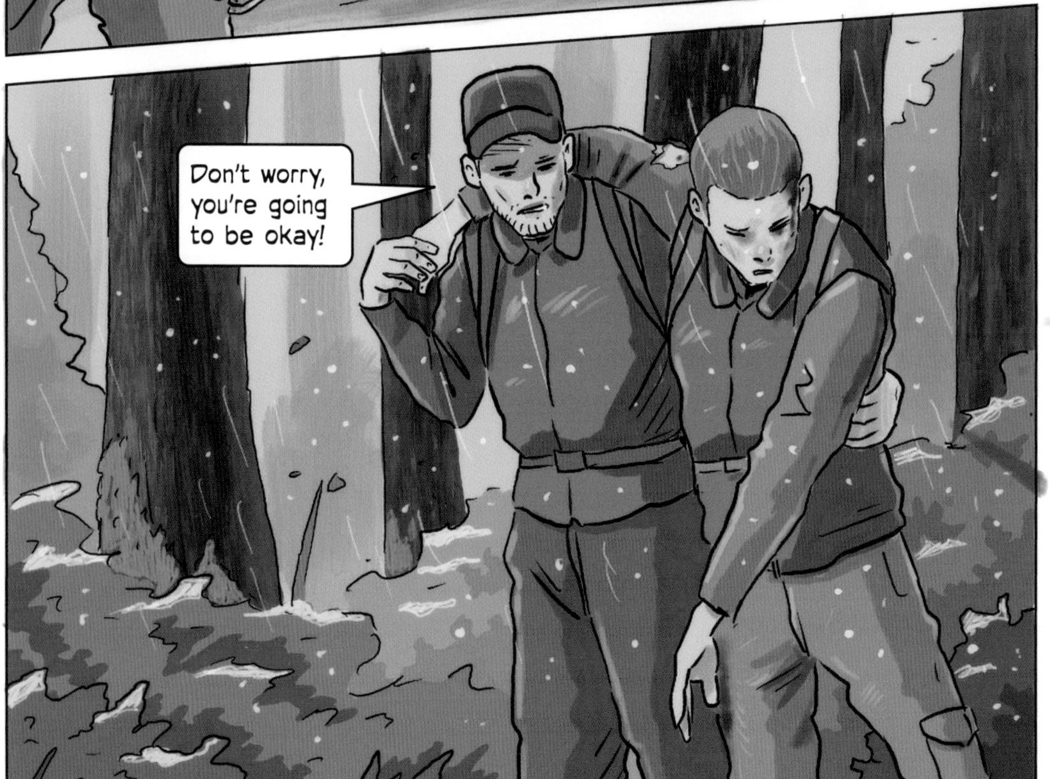
Don't worry, you're going to be okay!

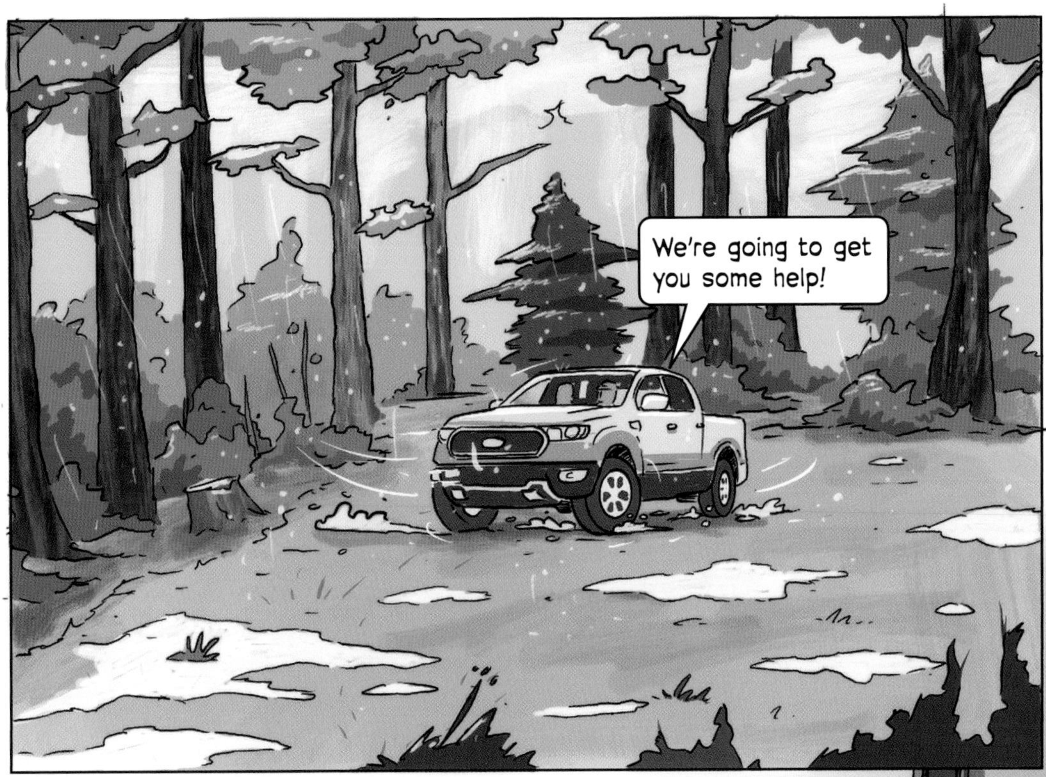
We're going to get you some help!

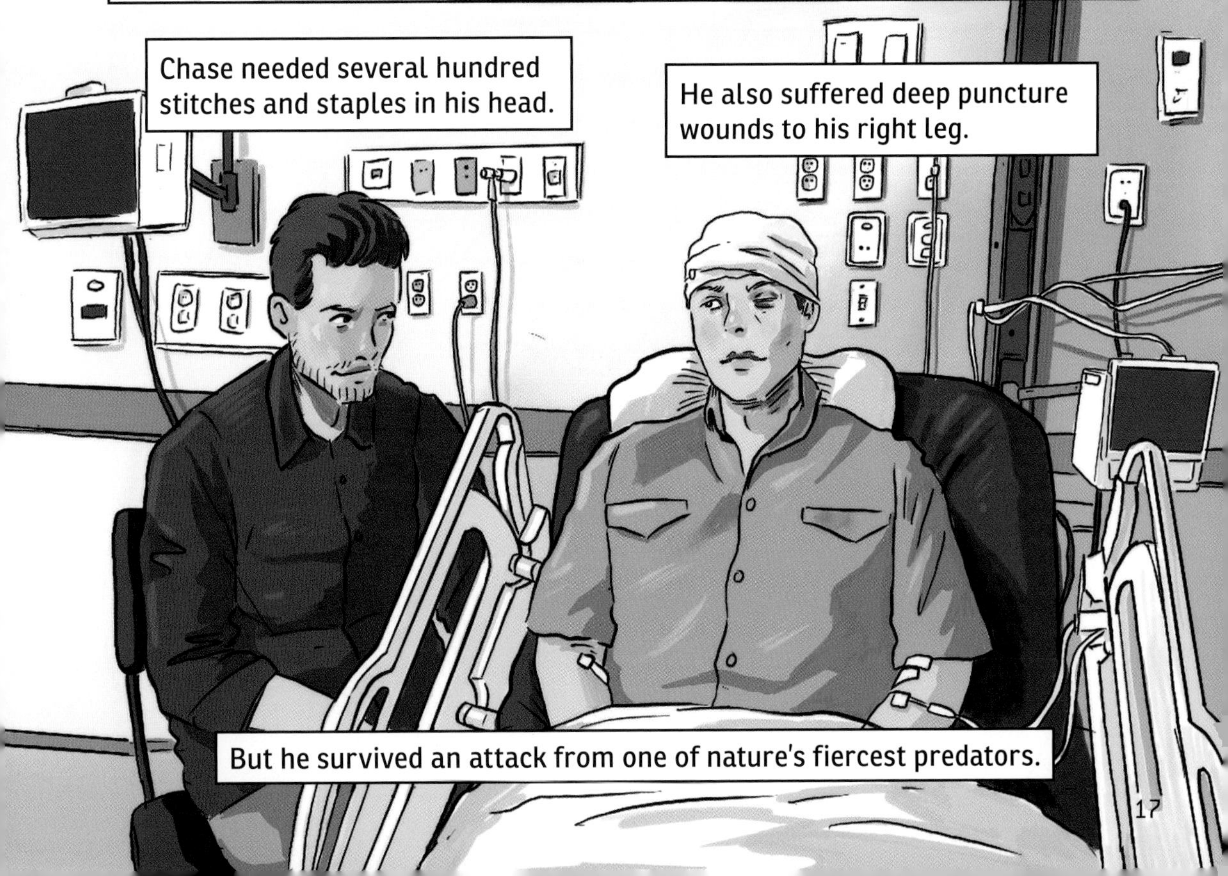
Chase needed several hundred stitches and staples in his head.
He also suffered deep puncture wounds to his right leg.
But he survived an attack from one of nature's fiercest predators.

CHAPTER 2
TERRITORIAL WATERS!

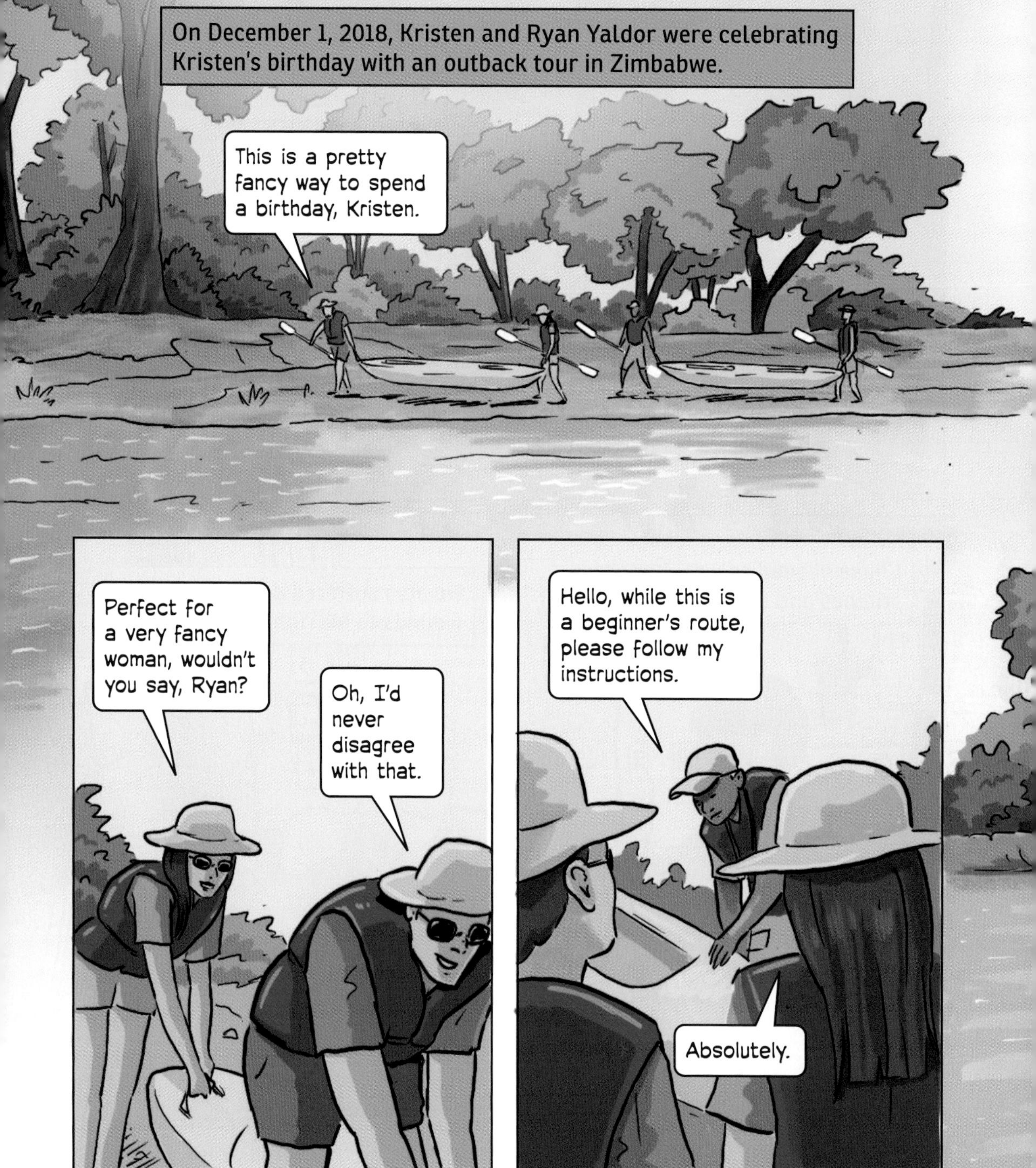
On December 1, 2018, Kristen and Ryan Yaldor were celebrating Kristen's birthday with an outback tour in Zimbabwe.
This is a pretty fancy way to spend a birthday, Kristen.
Perfect for a very fancy woman, wouldn't you say, Ryan?
Oh, I'd never disagree with that.
Hello, while this is a beginner's route, please follow my instructions.
Absolutely.

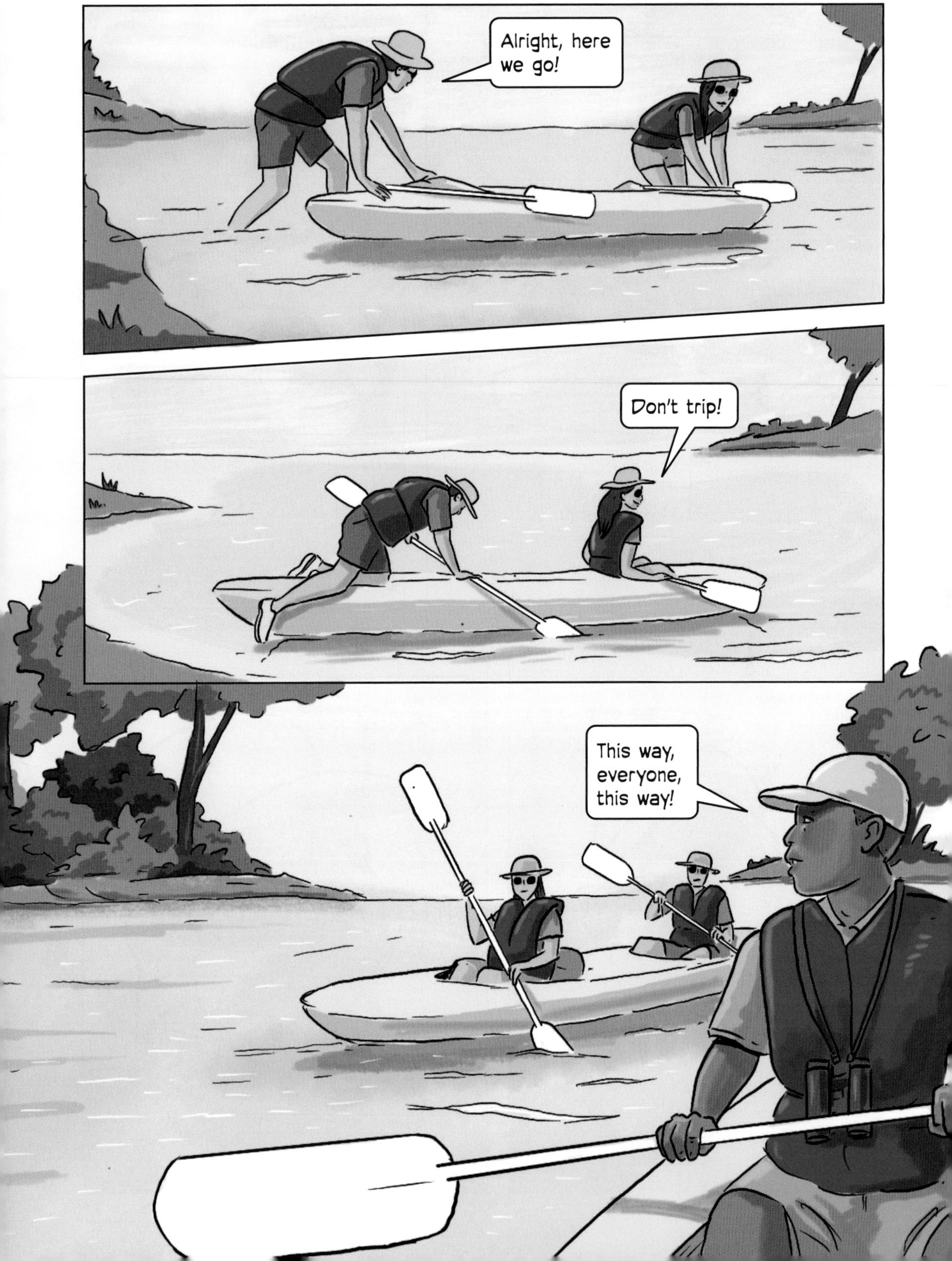
Alright, here we go!
Don't trip!
This way, everyone, this way!

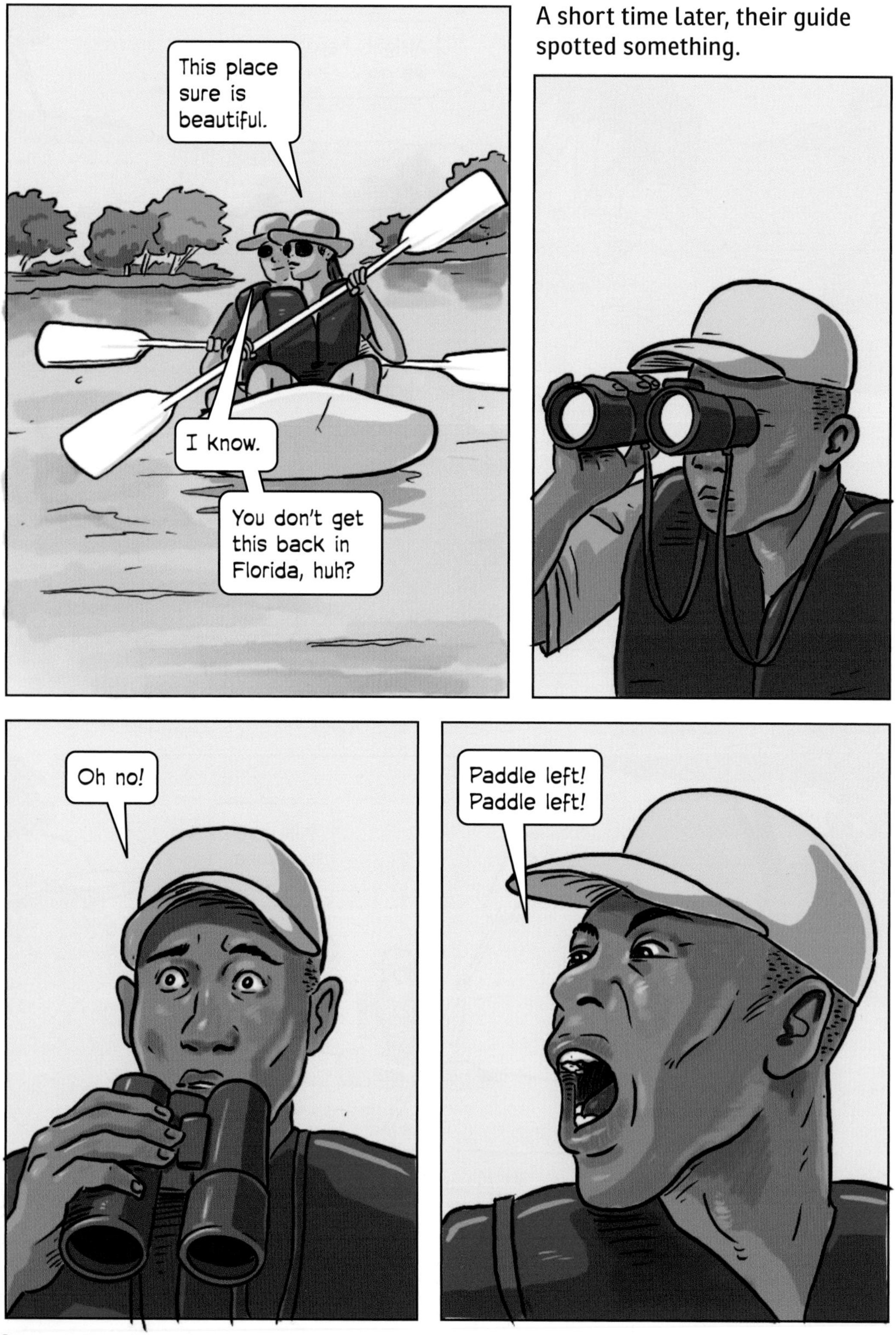
This place sure is beautiful.
I know.
You don't get this back in Florida, huh?
A short time later, their guide spotted something.
Oh no!
Paddle left! Paddle left!

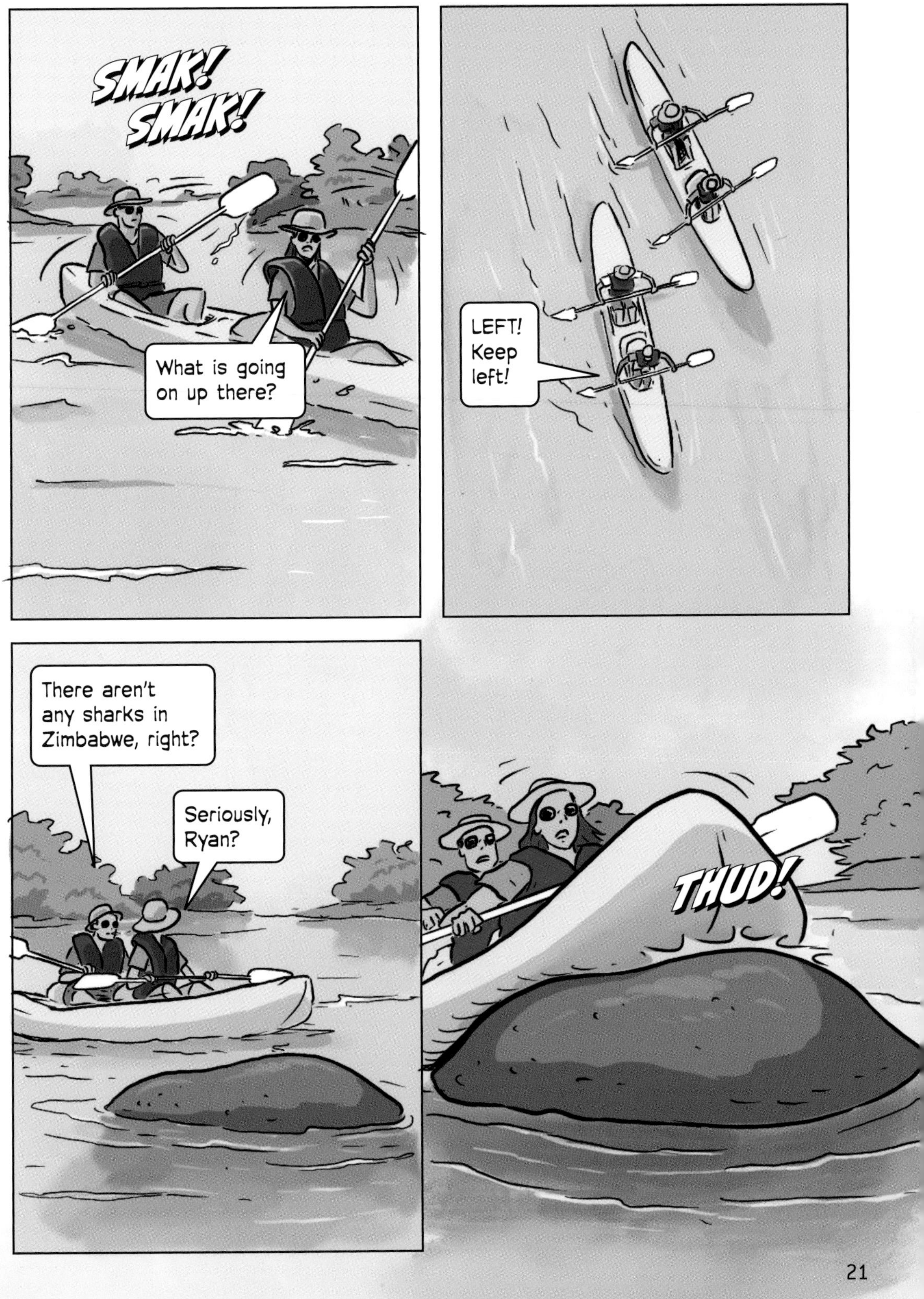
SMAK! SMAK!
What is going on up there?
LEFT! Keep left!
There aren't any sharks in Zimbabwe, right?
Seriously, Ryan?
THUD!

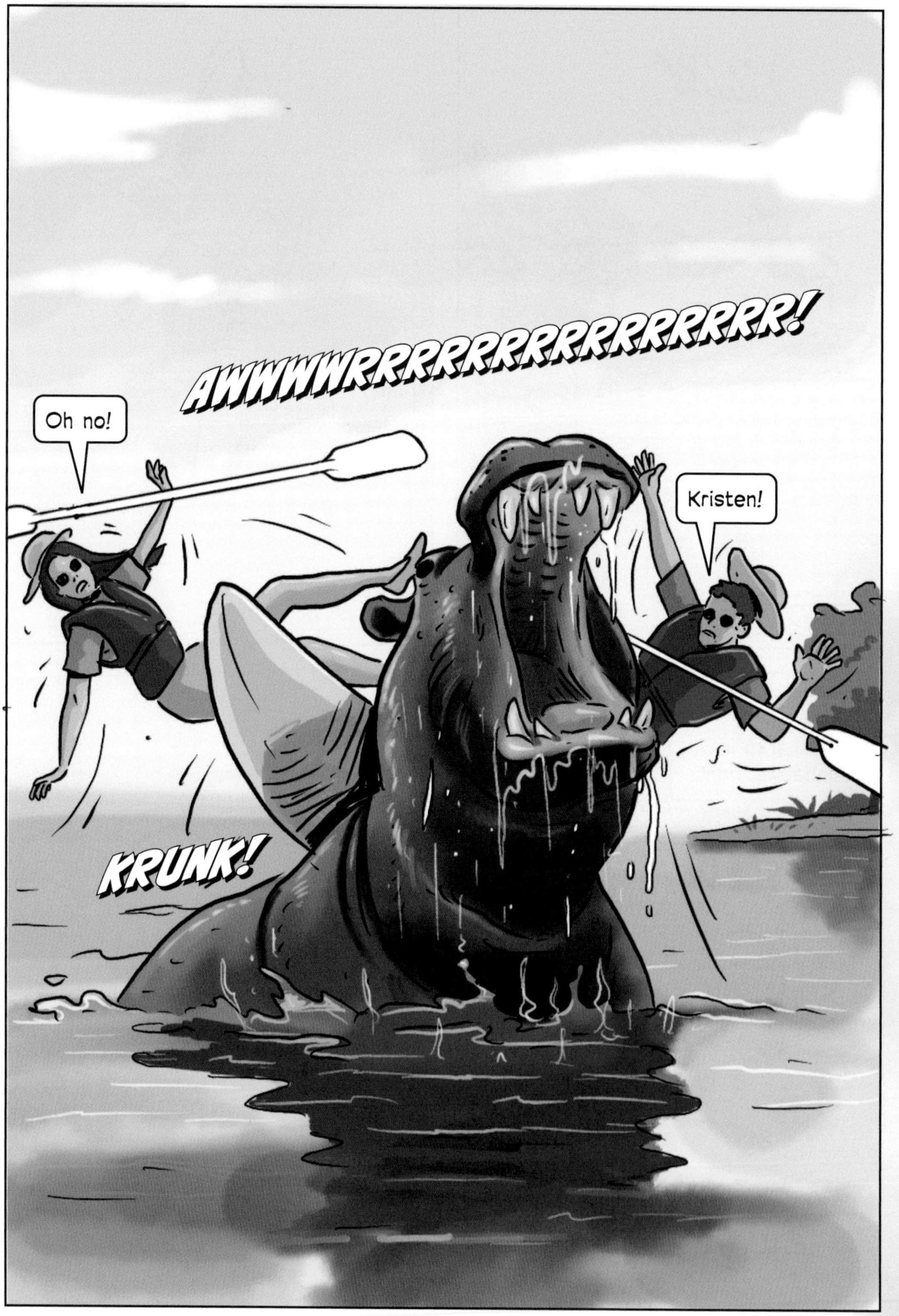
AWWWWRRRRRRRRRRRRRRR!
Oh no!
Kristen!
KRUNK!

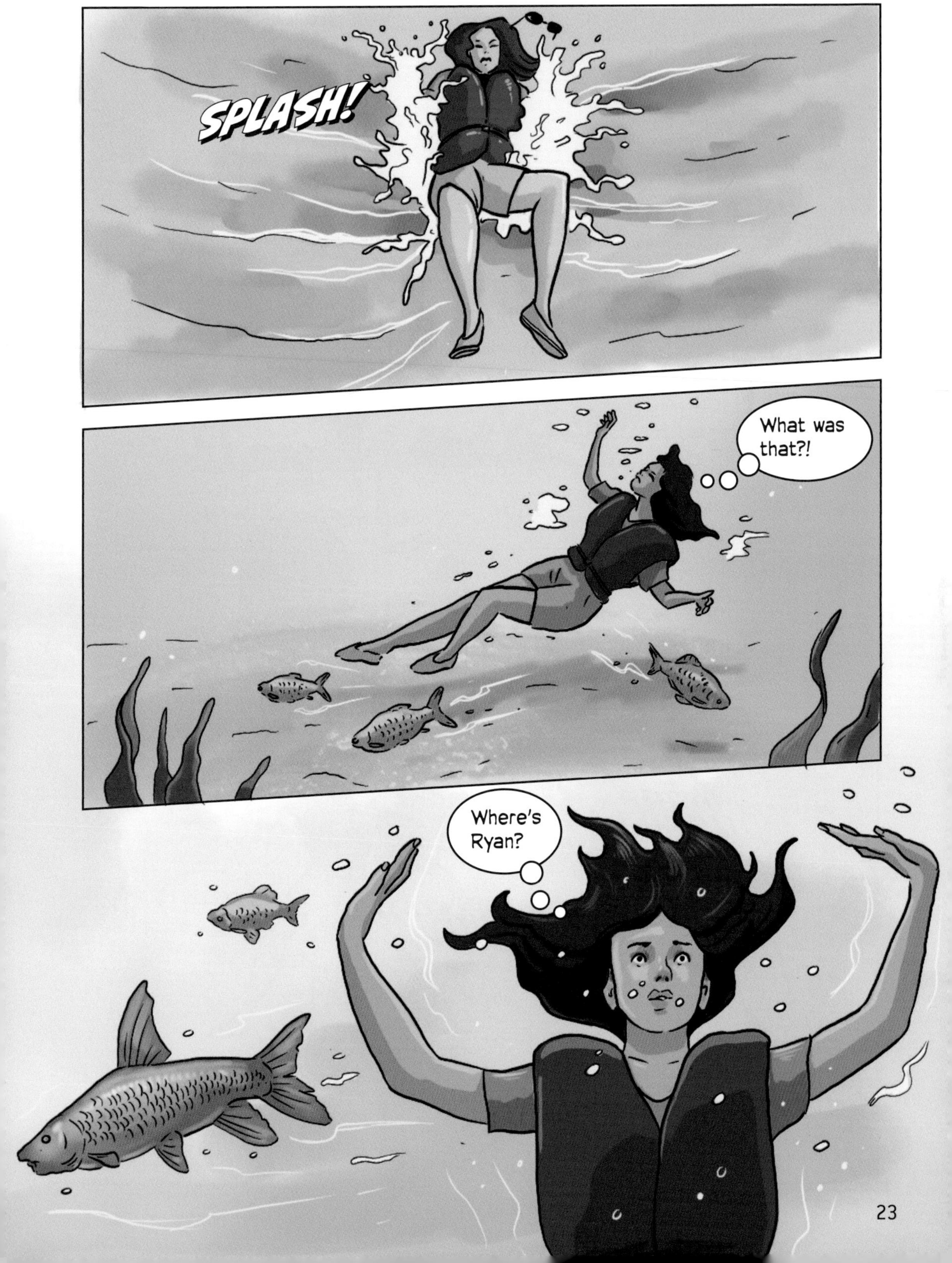
SPLASH!
What was that?!
Where's Ryan?

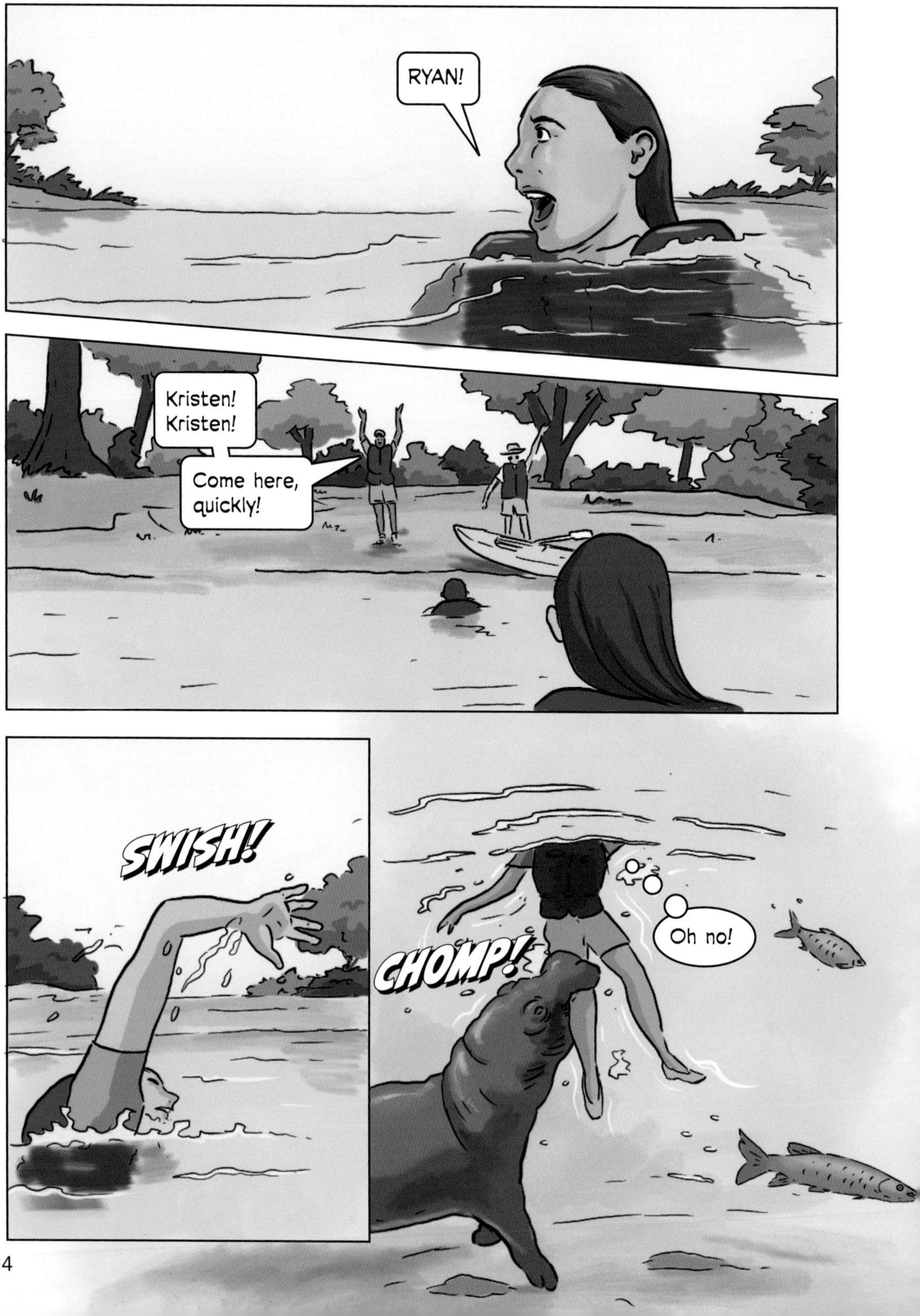
RYAN!
Kristen! Kristen!
Come here, quickly!
SWISH!
CHOMP!
Oh no!

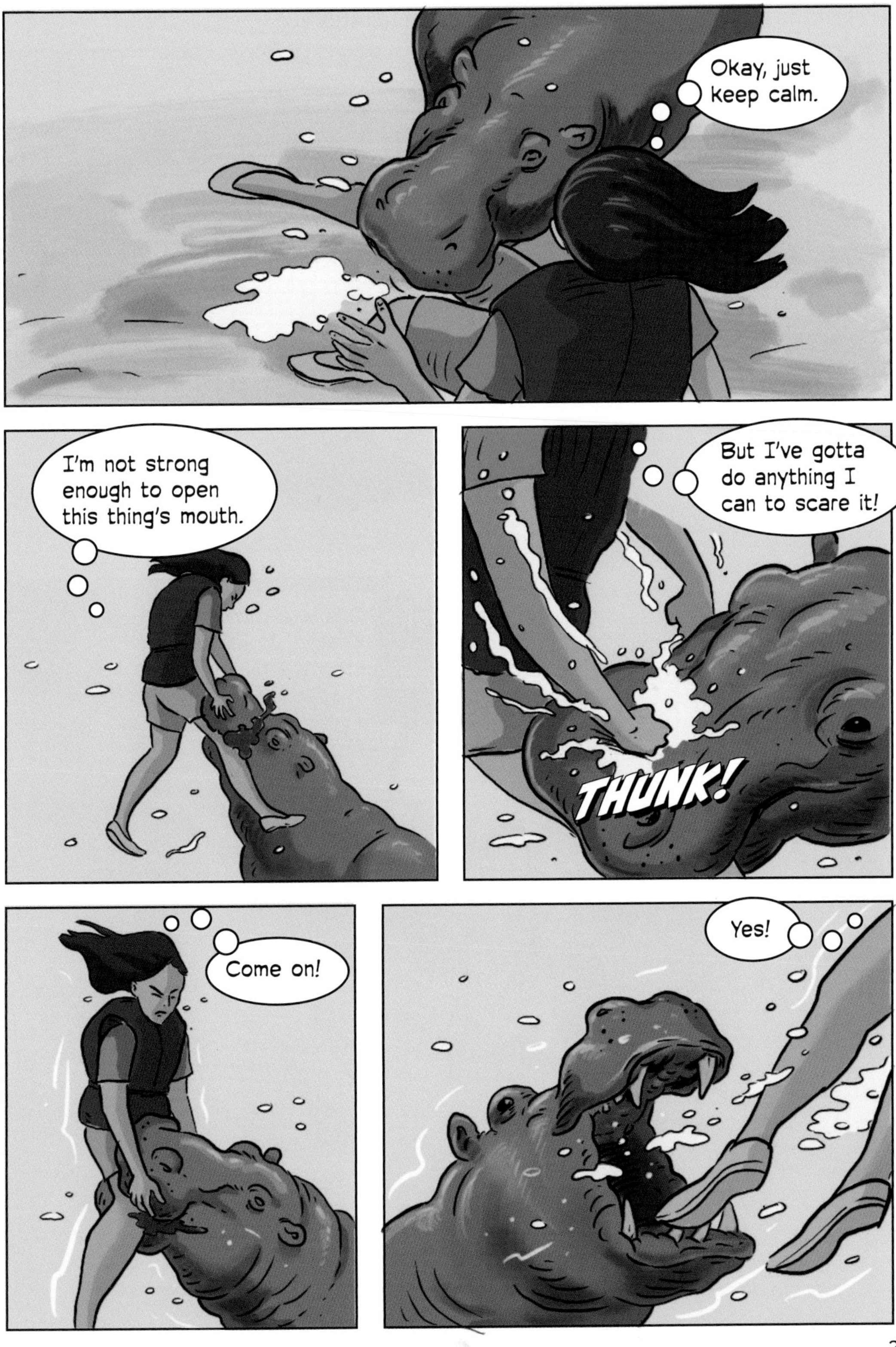

Okay, just keep calm.
I'm not strong enough to open this thing's mouth.
But I've gotta do anything I can to scare it!
THUNK!
Come on!
Yes!

Free of the hippo's jaws, Kristen quickly swam for shore.

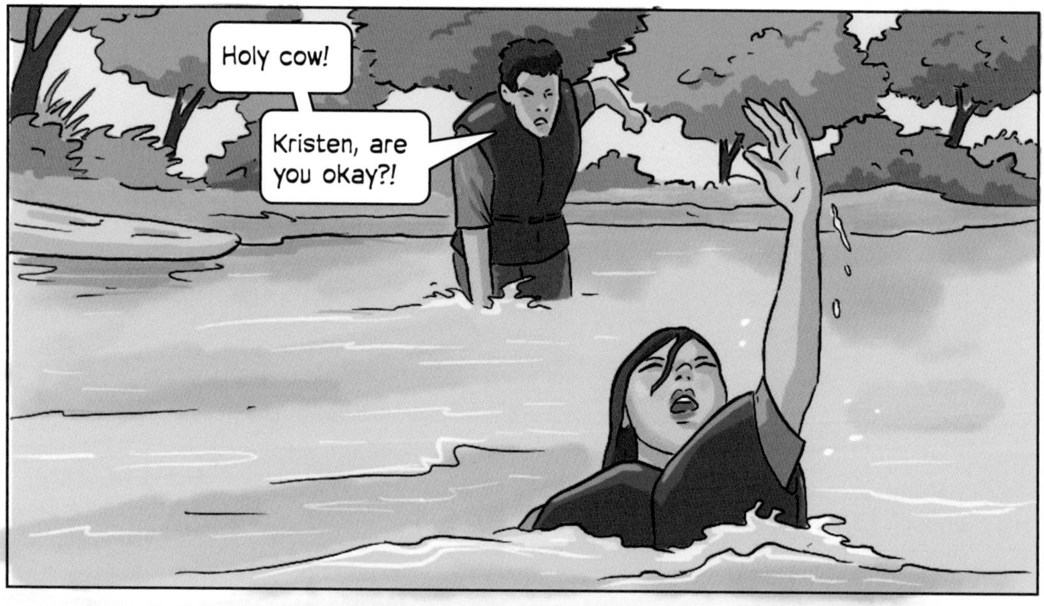

Holy cow!
Kristen, are you okay?!

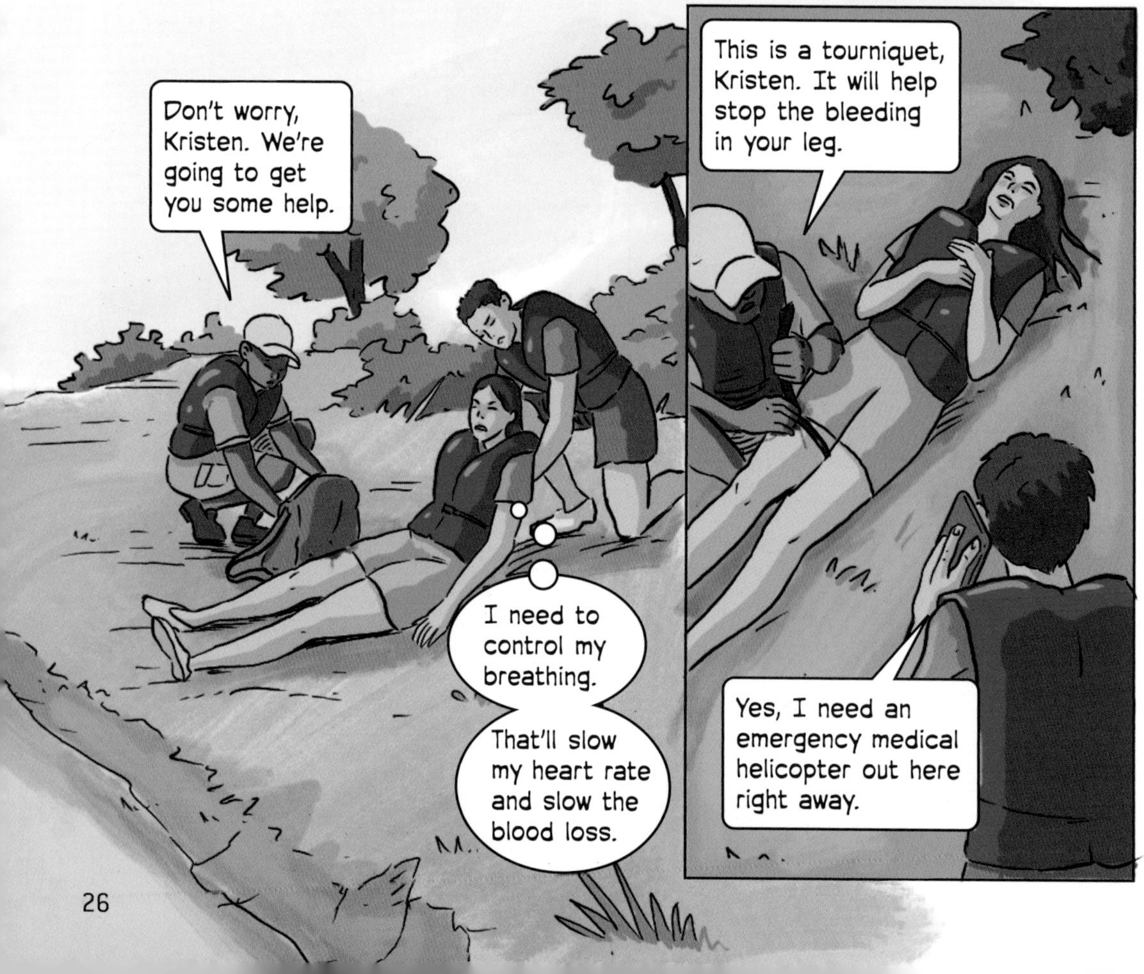

Don't worry, Kristen. We're going to get you some help.
I need to control my breathing.
That'll slow my heart rate and slow the blood loss.
This is a tourniquet, Kristen. It will help stop the bleeding in your leg.
Yes, I need an emergency medical helicopter out here right away.

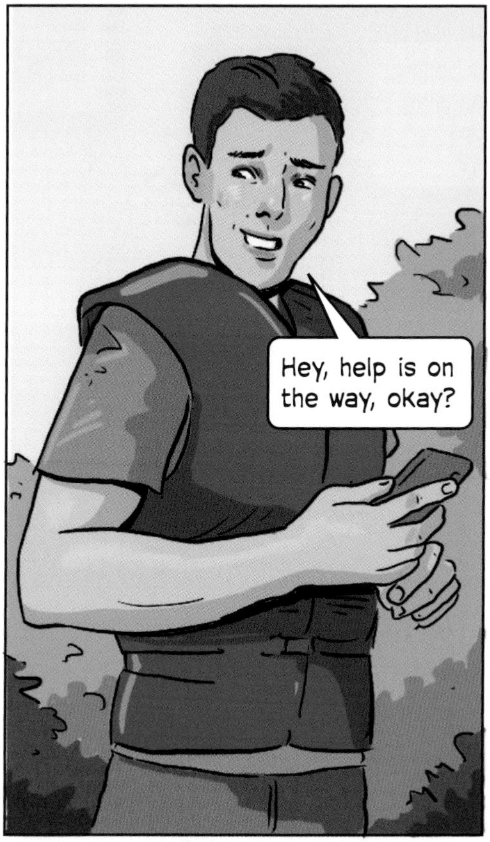
Hey, help is on the way, okay?

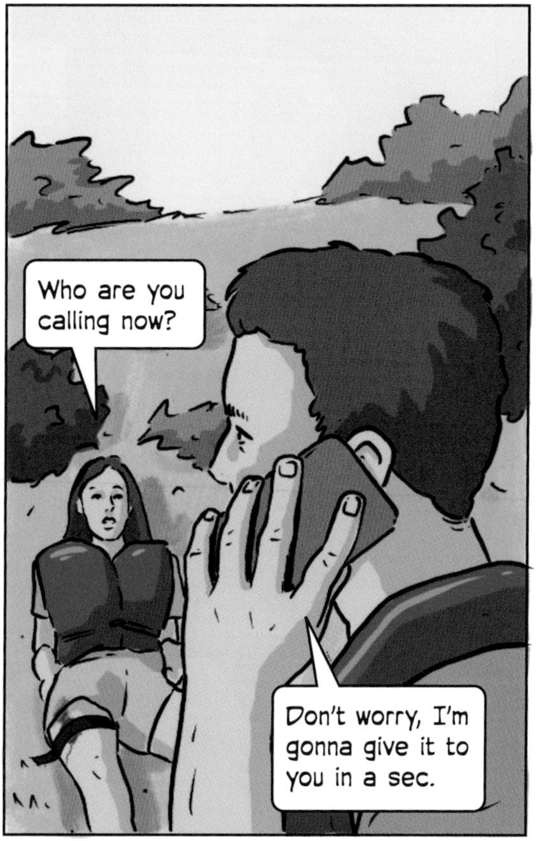
Who are you calling now?
Don't worry, I'm gonna give it to you in a sec.

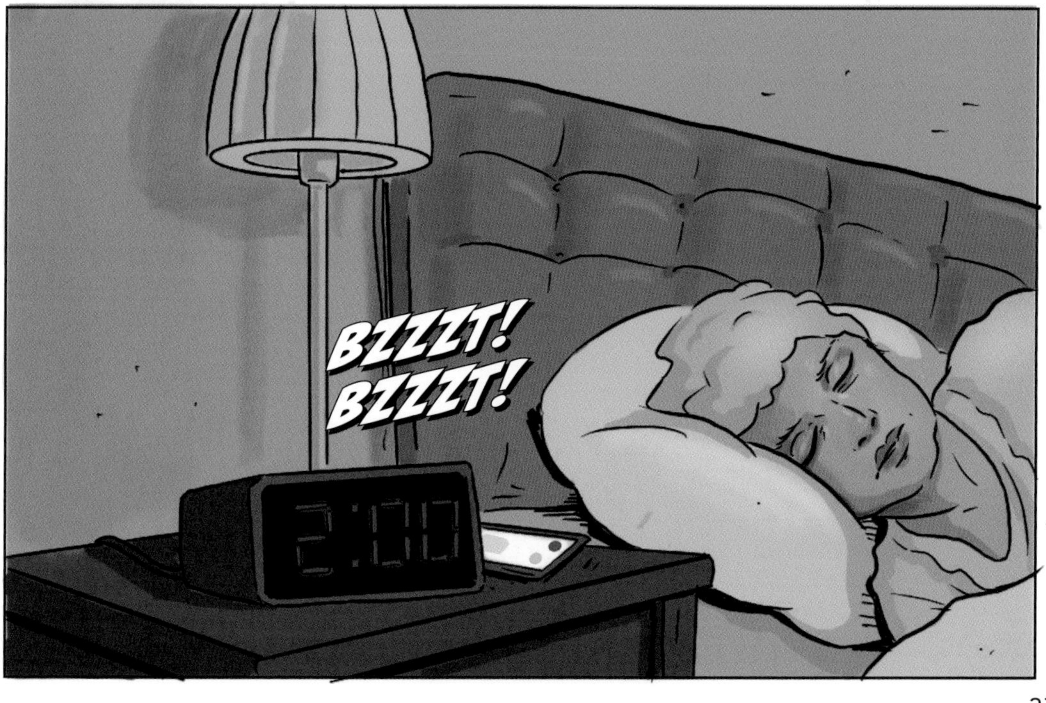
BZZZT! BZZZT!

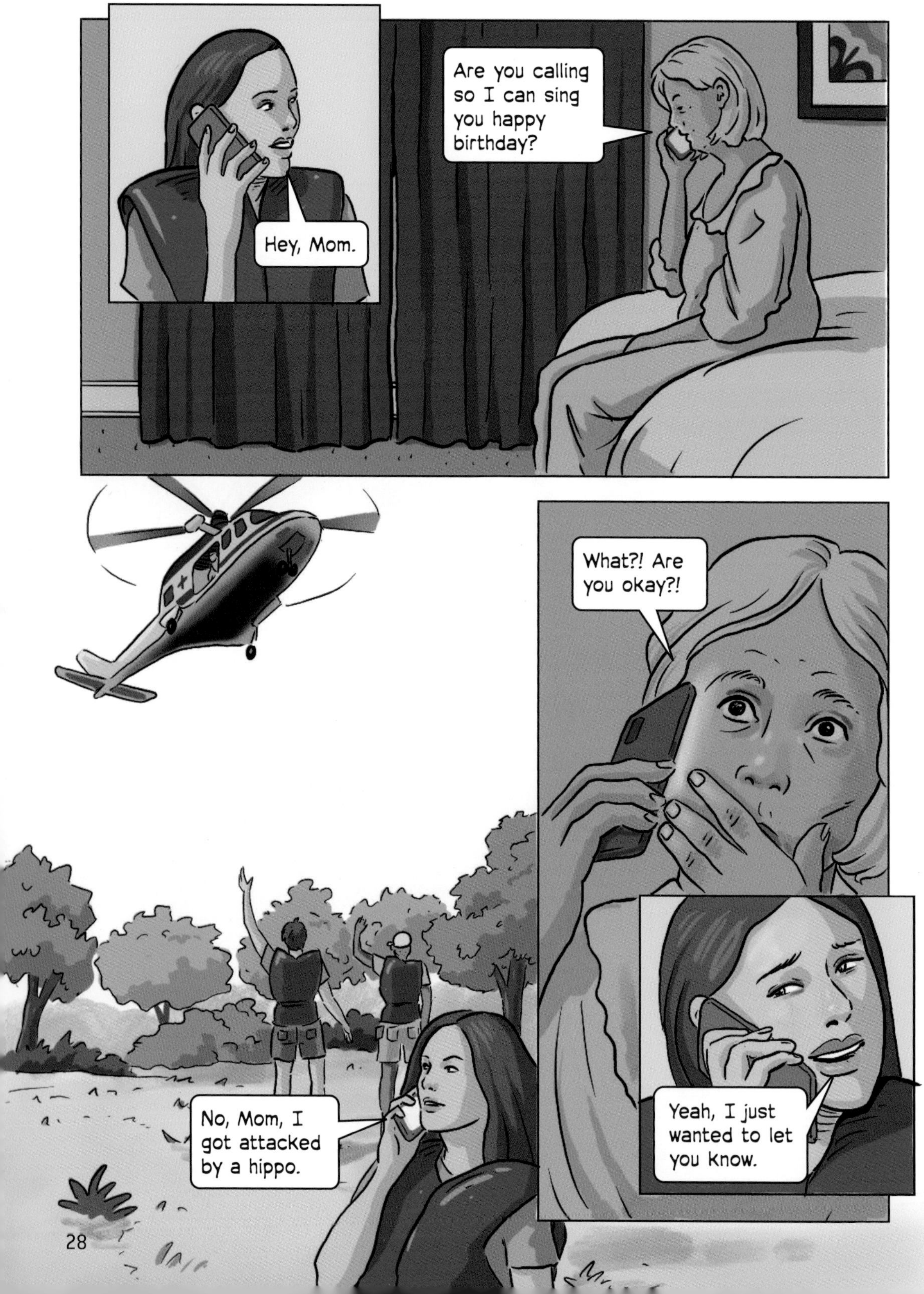
Hey, Mom.
Are you calling so I can sing you happy birthday?
No, Mom, I got attacked by a hippo.
What?! Are you okay?!
Yeah, I just wanted to let you know.

The hippo attack left Kristen with a broken femur and a mangled leg.

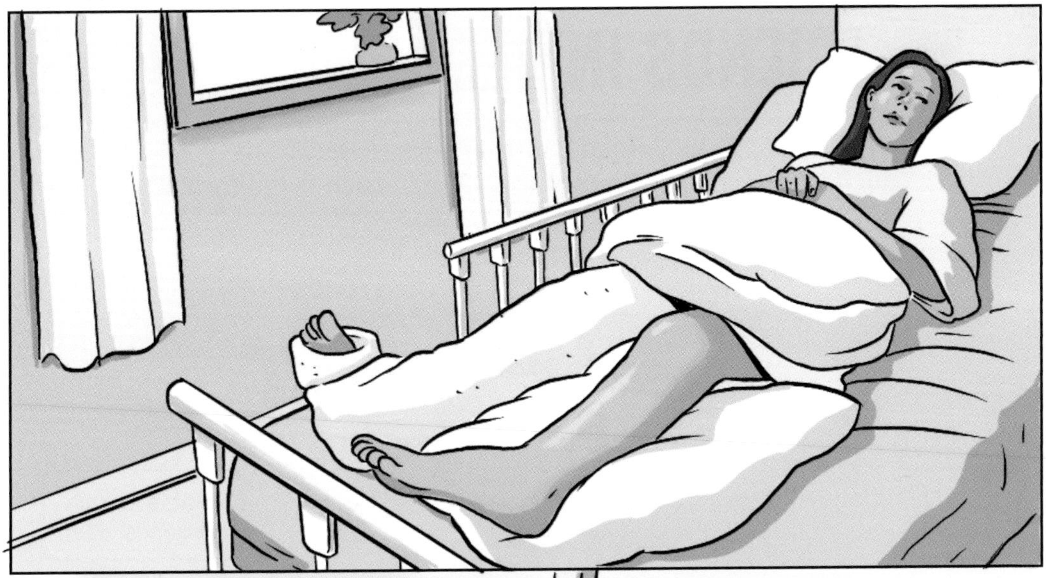

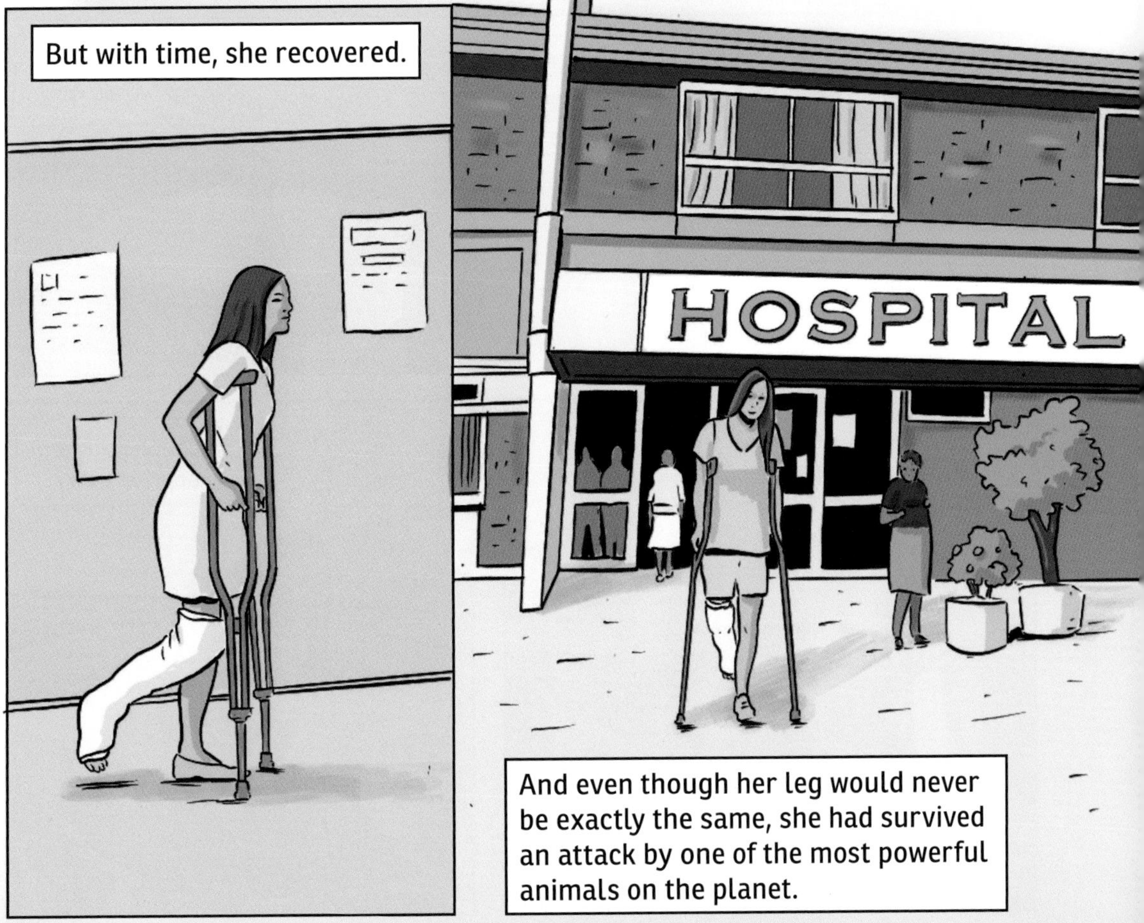
But with time, she recovered.
HOSPITAL
And even though her leg would never be exactly the same, she had survived an attack by one of the most powerful animals on the planet.

CHAPTER 3
FRIENDS IN DEEP PLACES!

On August 28, 2007, Todd Endris and his friends went surfing at Monterey Bay's Marina State Beach in California.

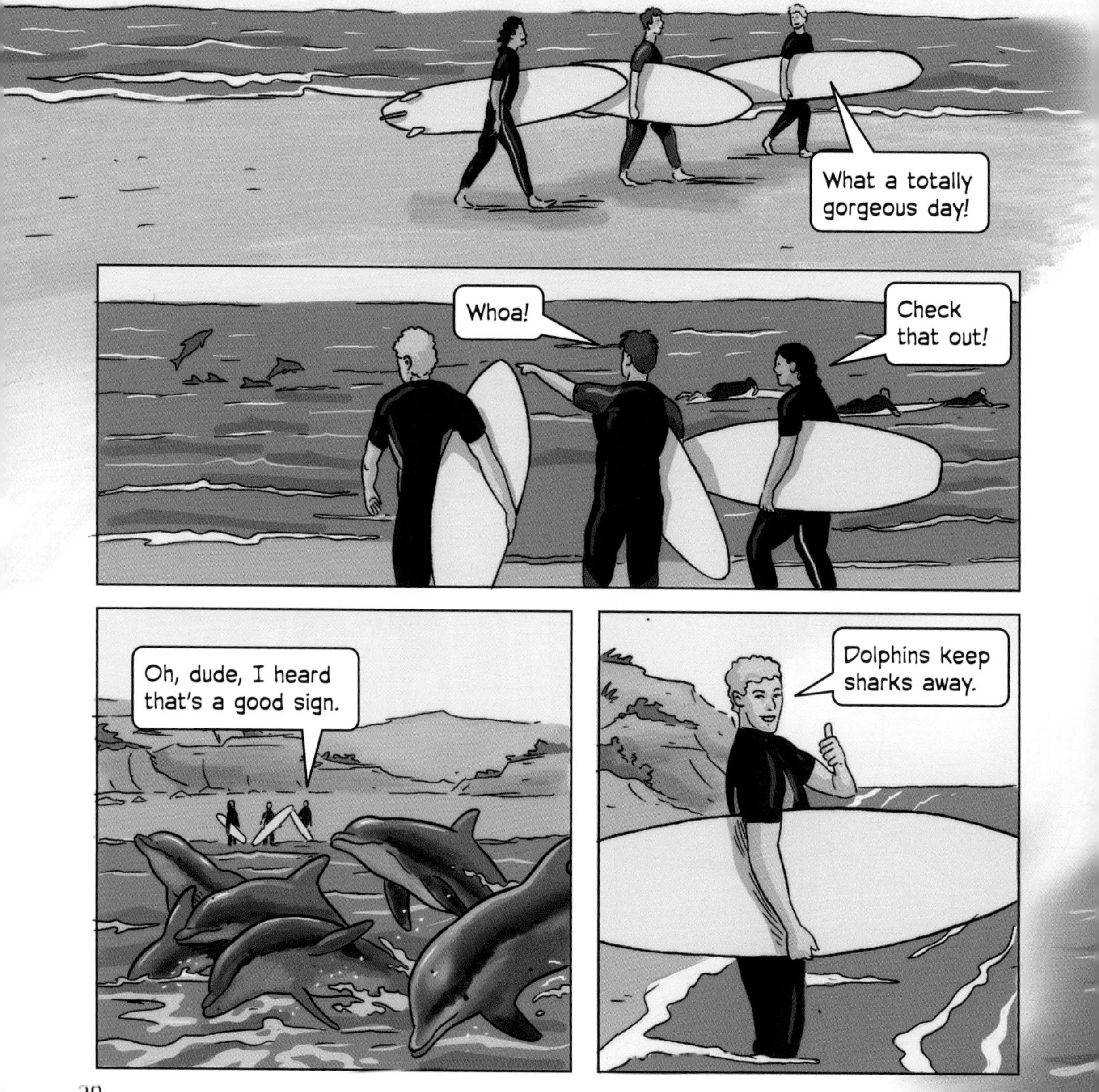

What a totally gorgeous day!
Whoa!
Check that out!
Oh, dude, I heard that's a good sign.
Dolphins keep sharks away.

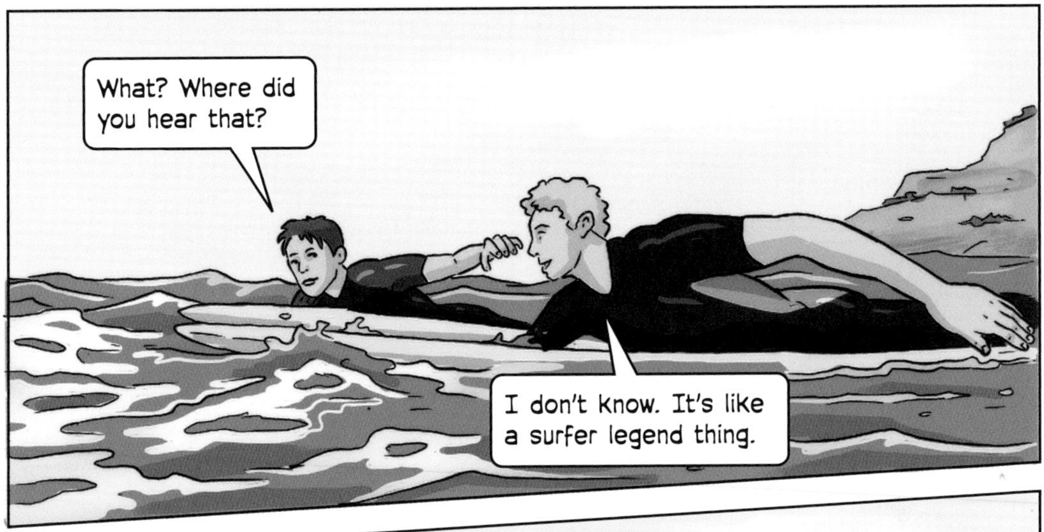
What? Where did you hear that?
I don't know. It's like a surfer legend thing.
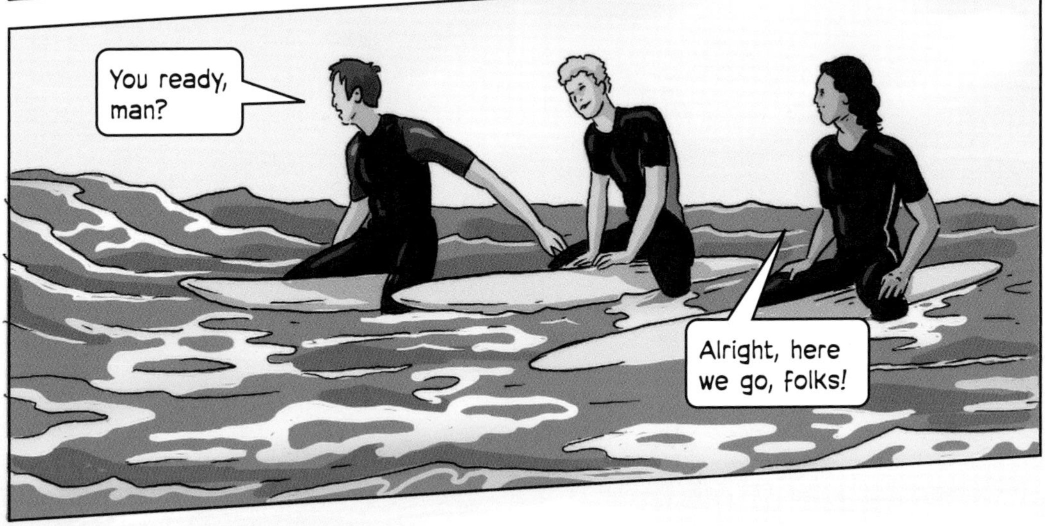
You ready, man?
Alright, here we go, folks!
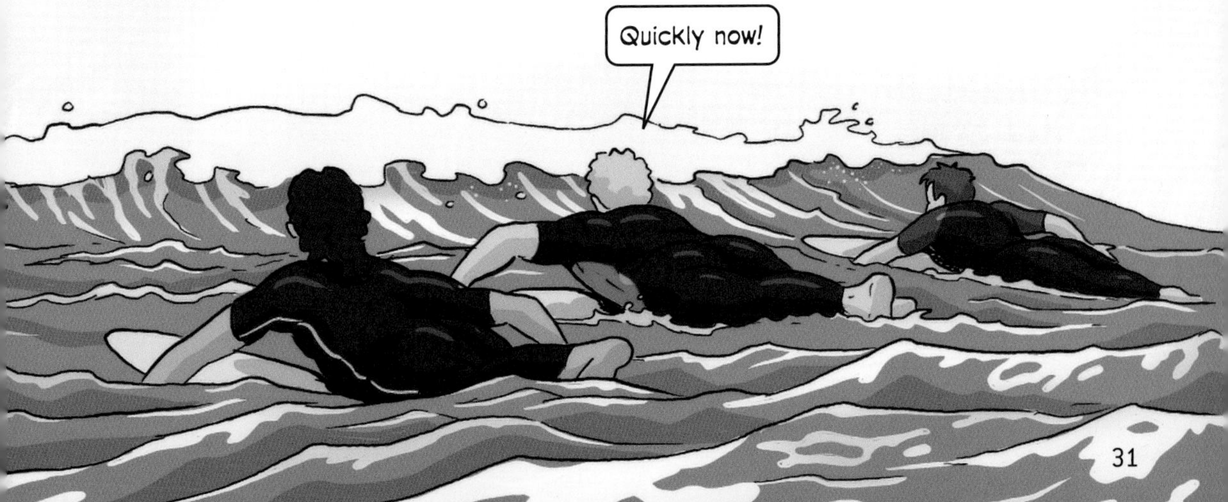
Quickly now!

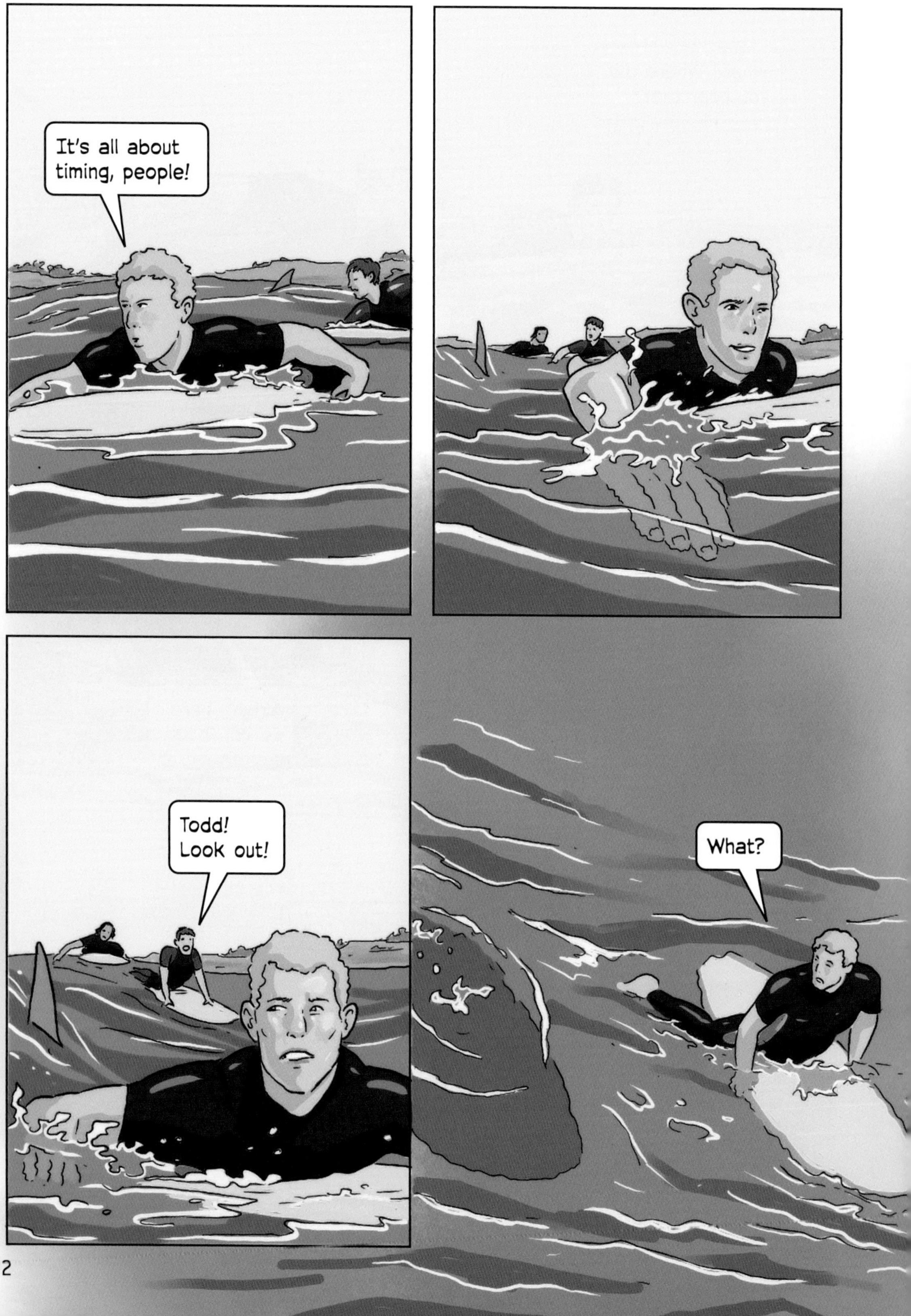
It's all about timing, people!
Todd! Look out!
What?

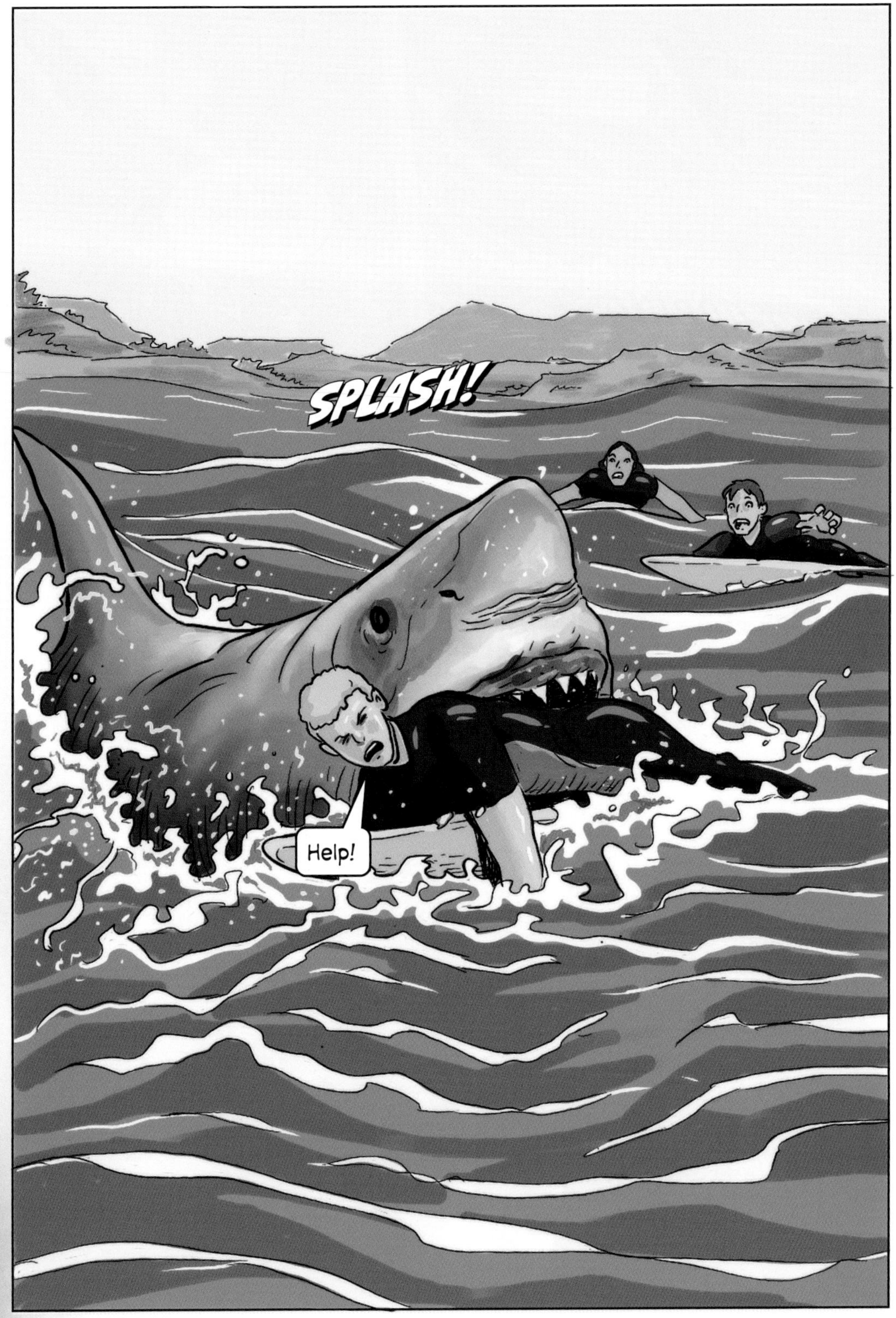
SPLASH!
Help!

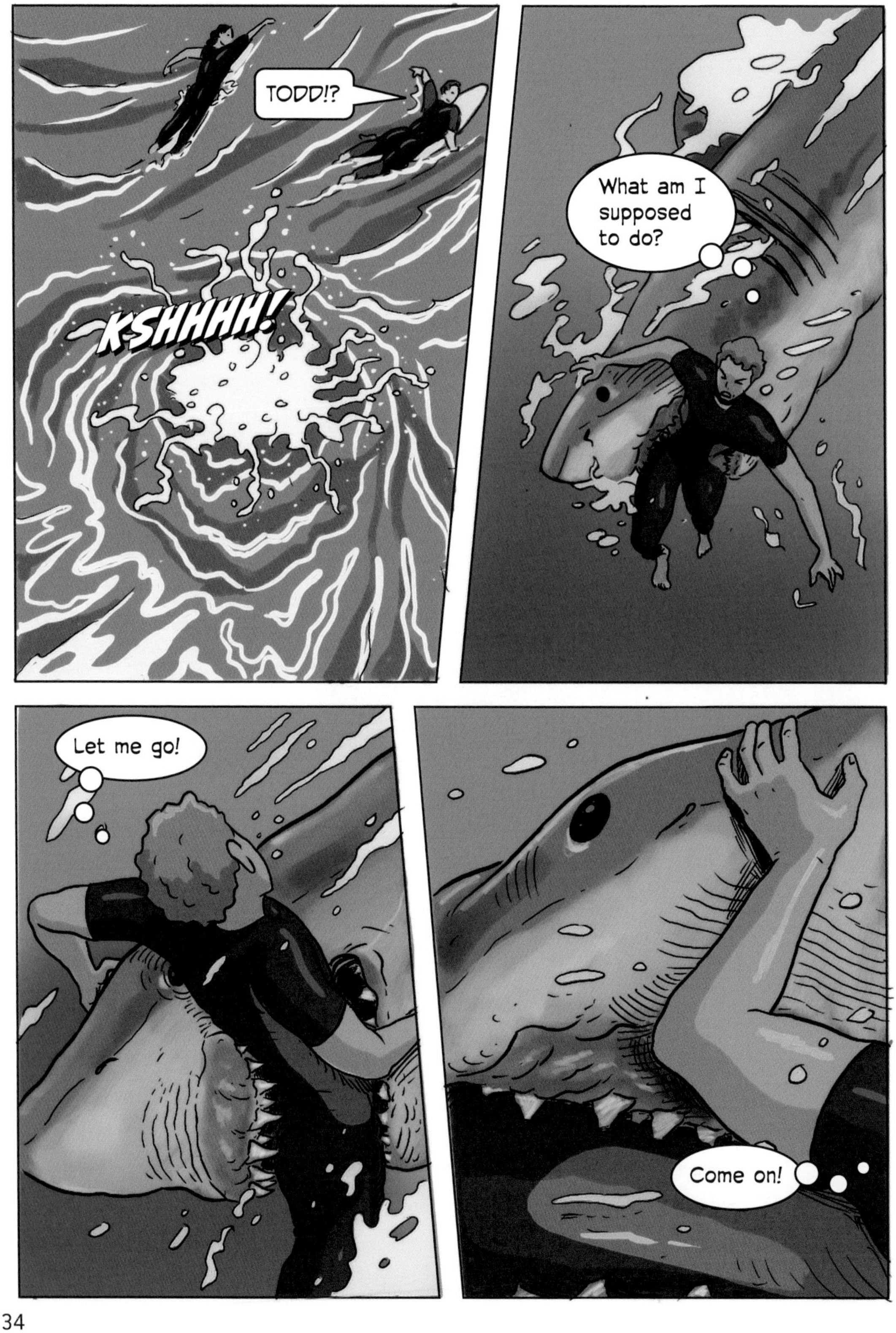
TODD!?
KSHHHH!
What am I supposed to do?
Let me go!
Come on!

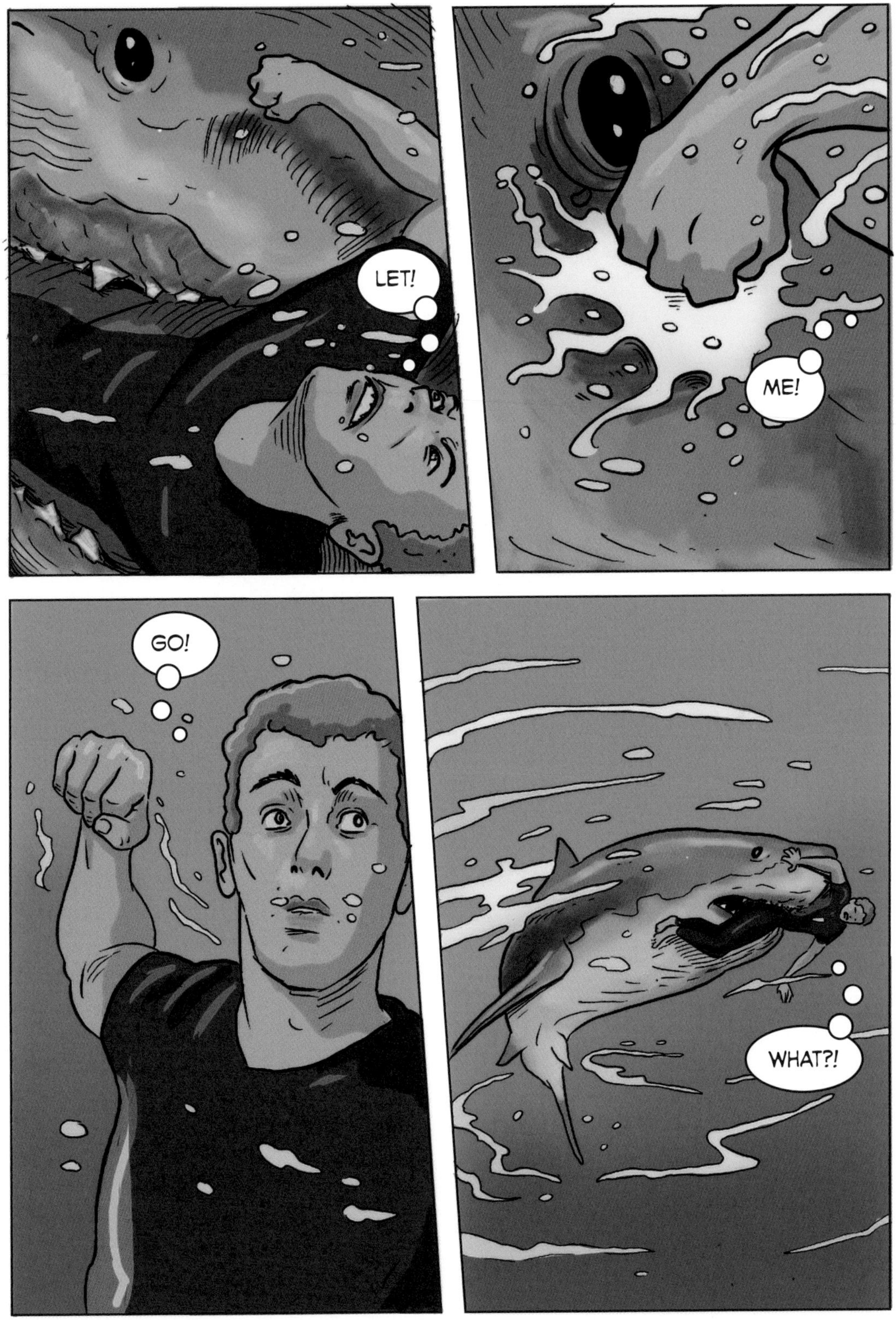
LET!
ME!
GO!
WHAT?!

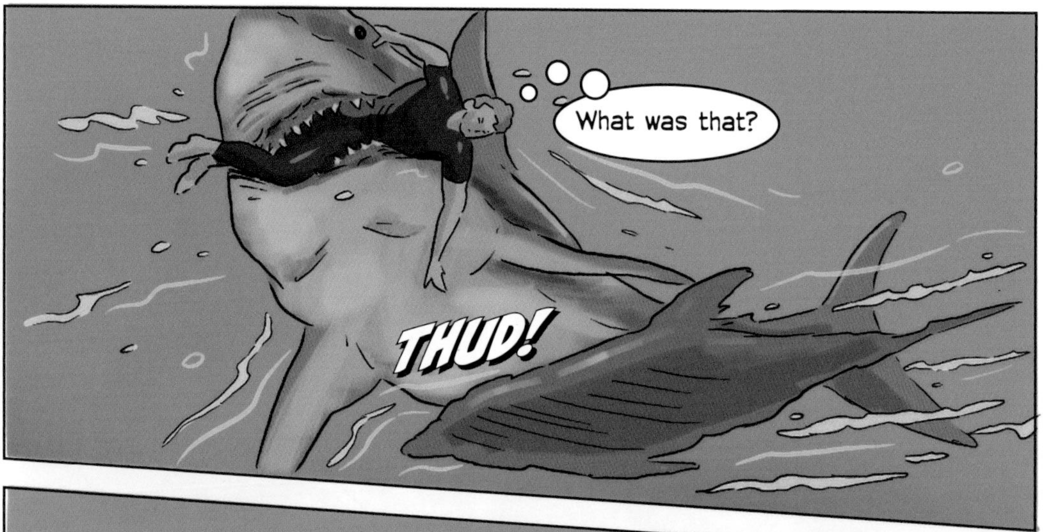
What was that?
THUD!

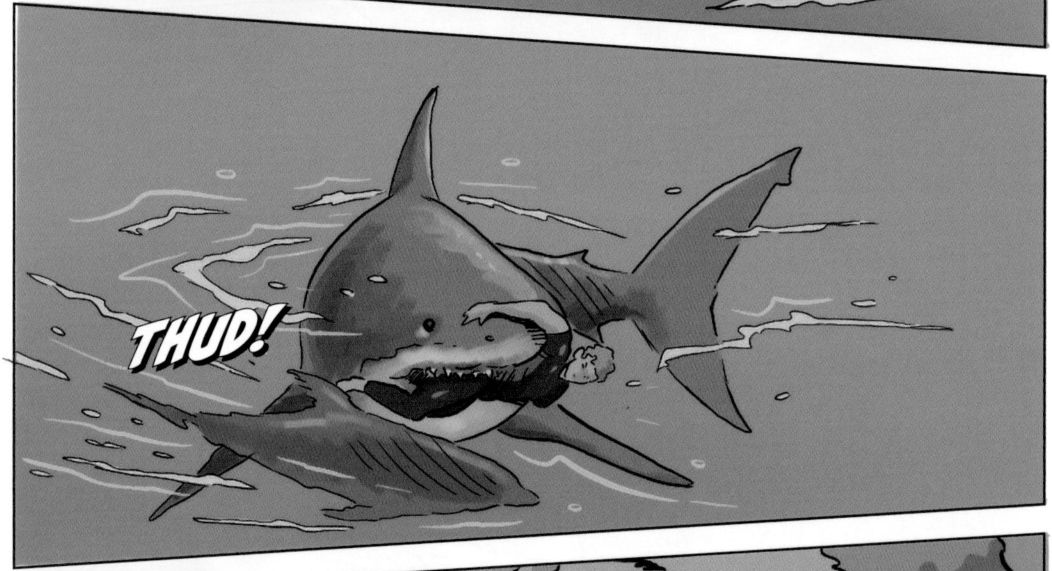
THUD!

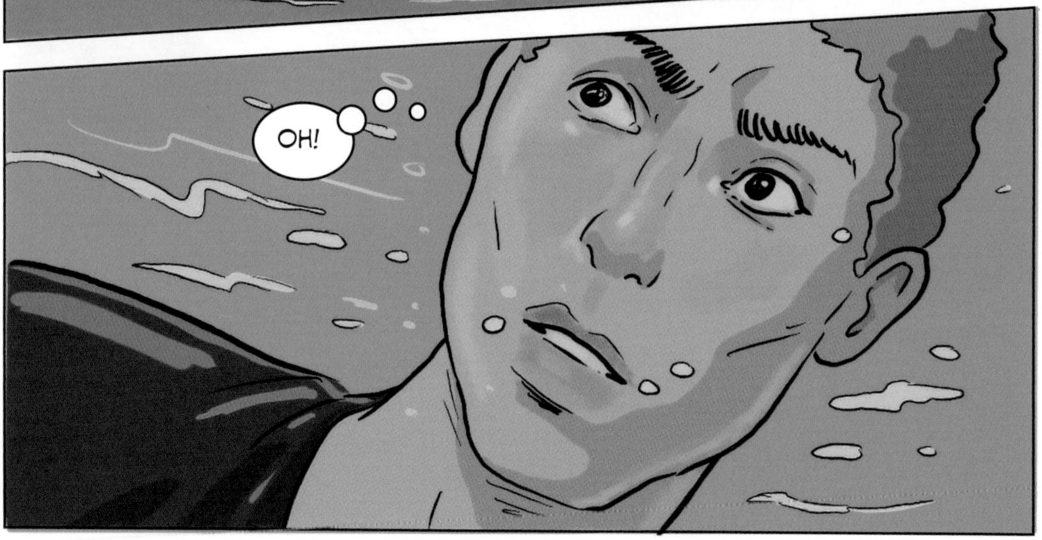
OH!

Much to Todd's surprise, the pod of dolphins had come to his rescue!

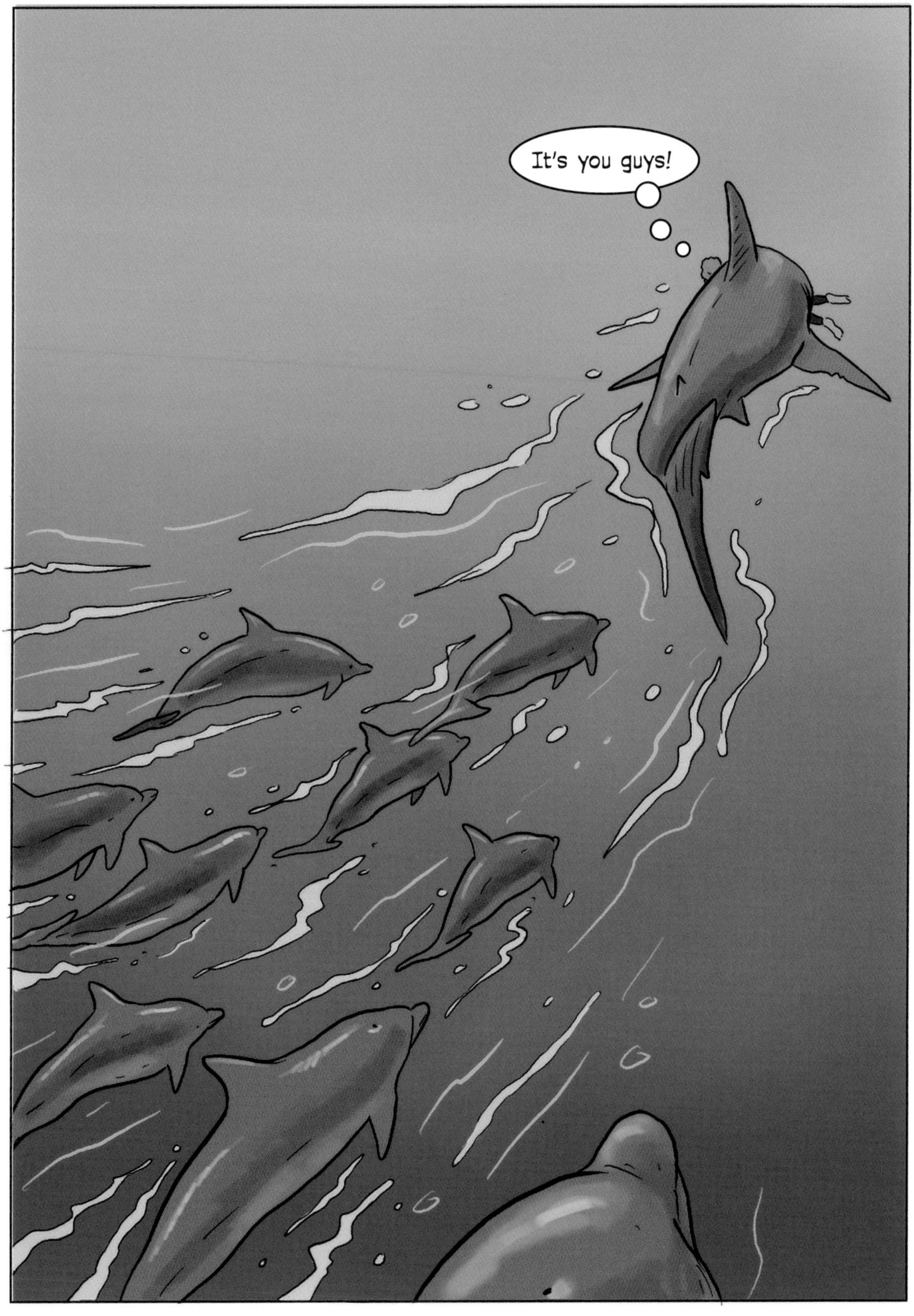
It's you guys!

Working together, the dolphins rammed the shark.

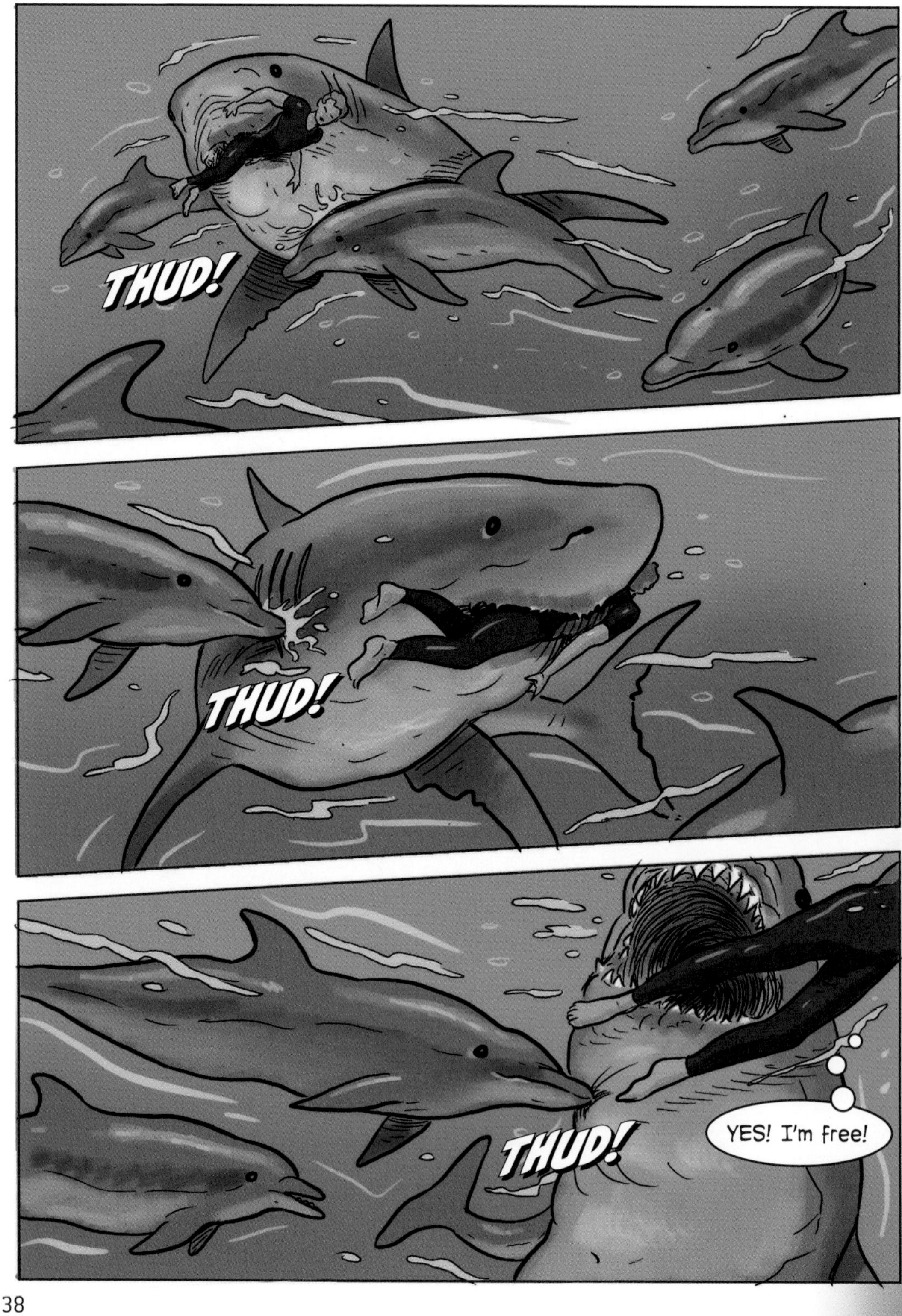
THUD!
THUD!
THUD!
YES! I'm free!

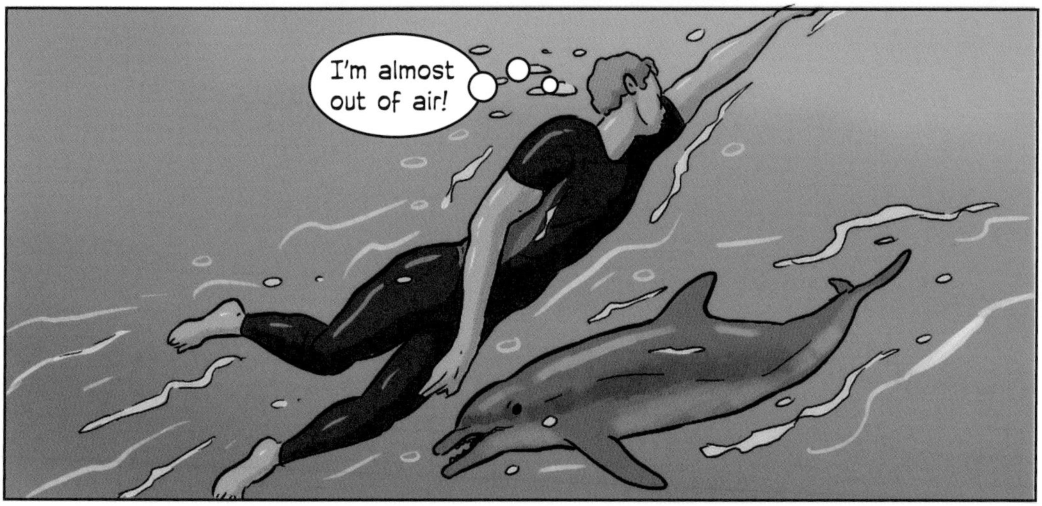
I'm almost out of air!

Then they formed a wall to protect Todd.

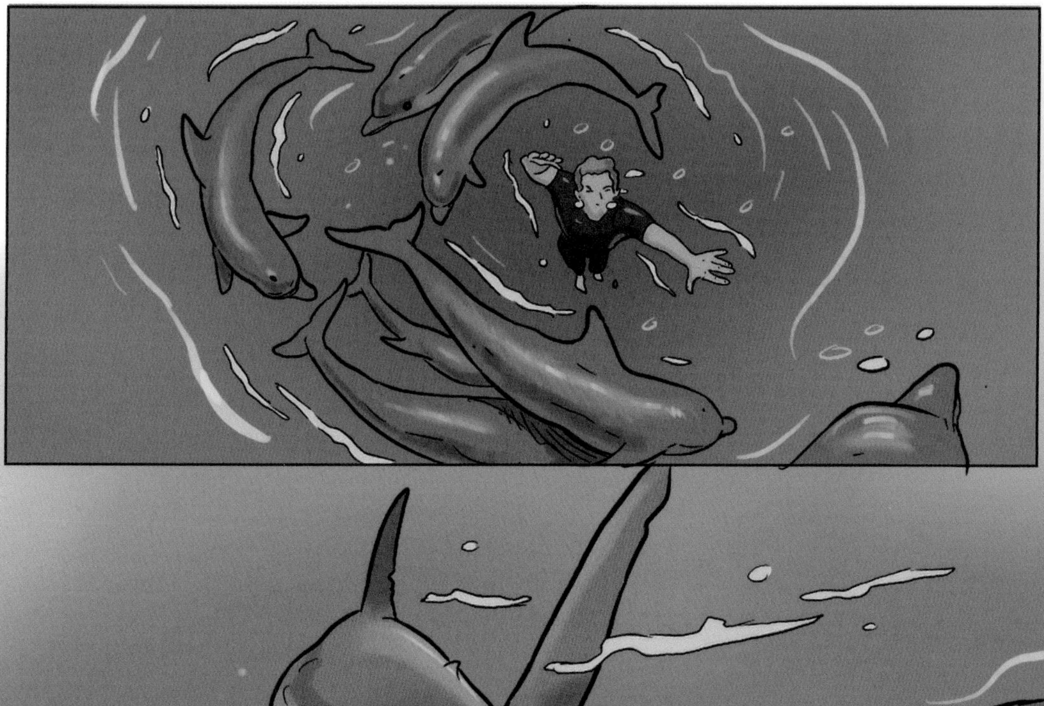

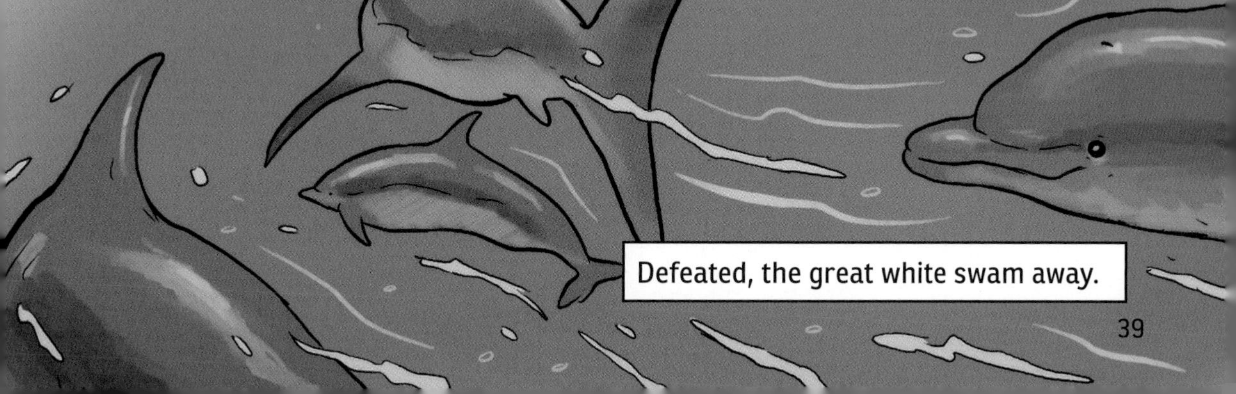
Defeated, the great white swam away.

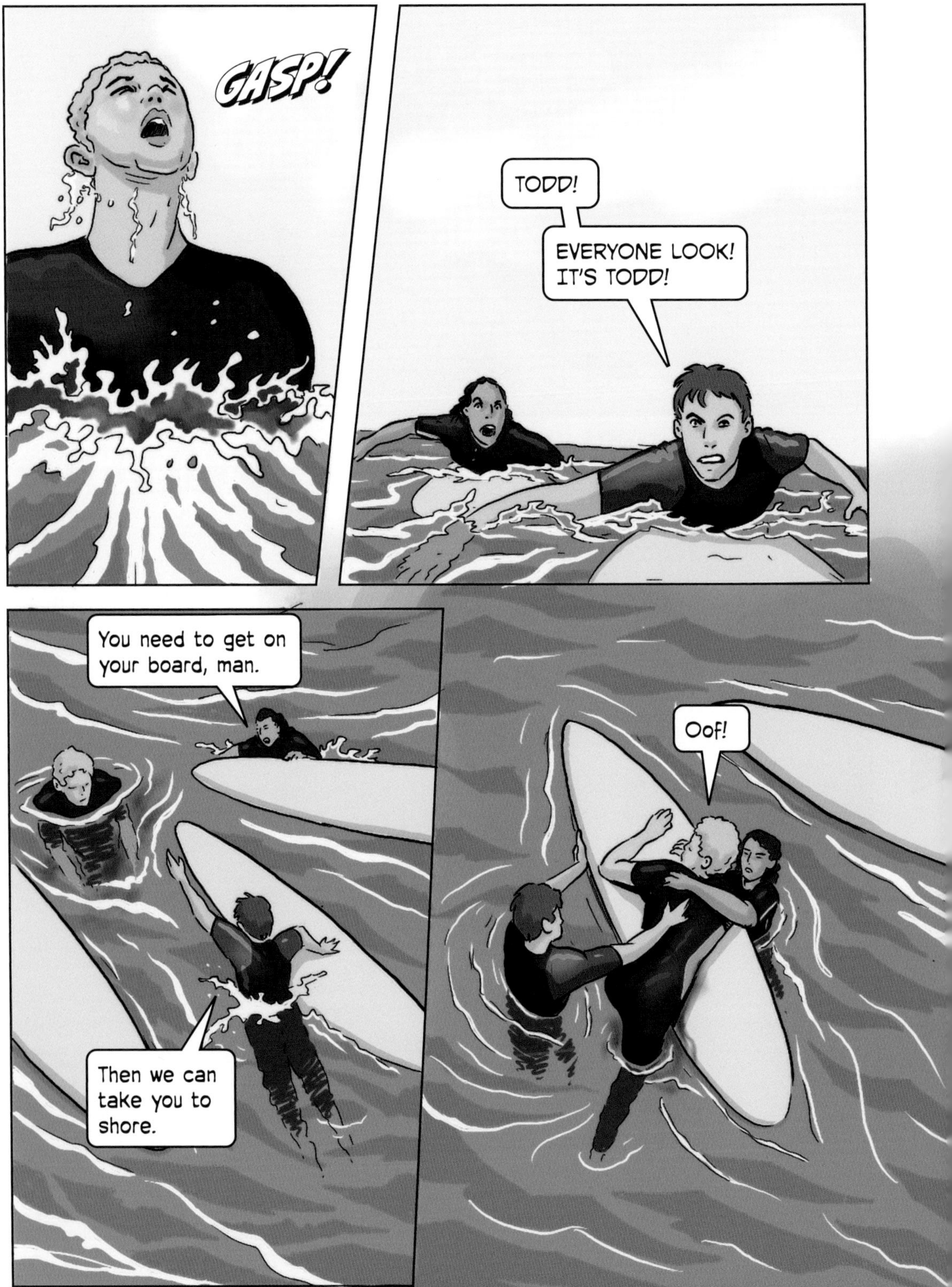
GASP!
TODD!
EVERYONE LOOK! IT'S TODD!
You need to get on your board, man.
Then we can take you to shore.
Oof!

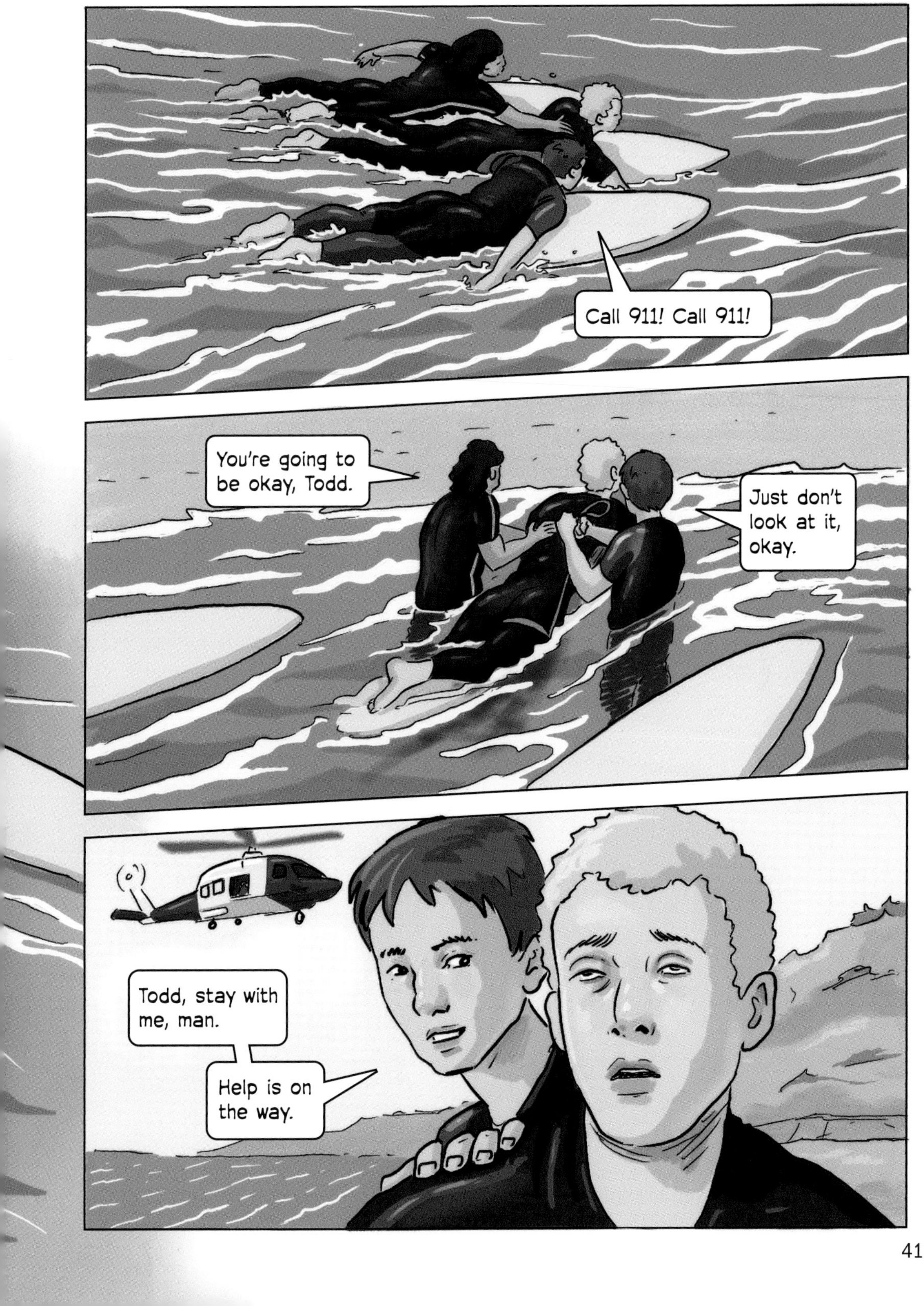
Call 911! Call 911!
You're going to be okay, Todd.
Just don't look at it, okay.
Todd, stay with me, man.
Help is on the way.

Todd's injuries were severe.

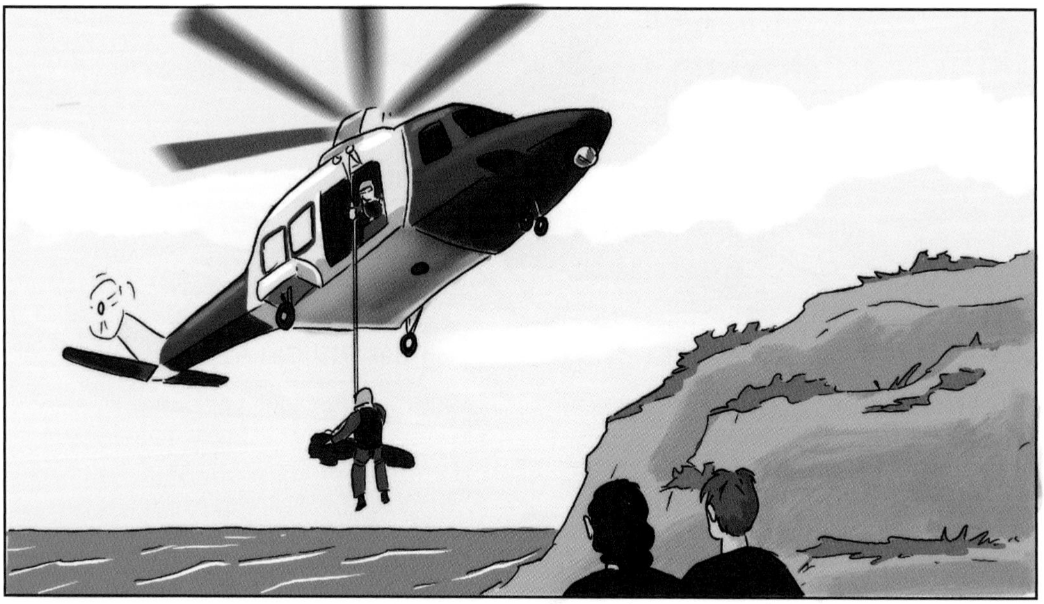

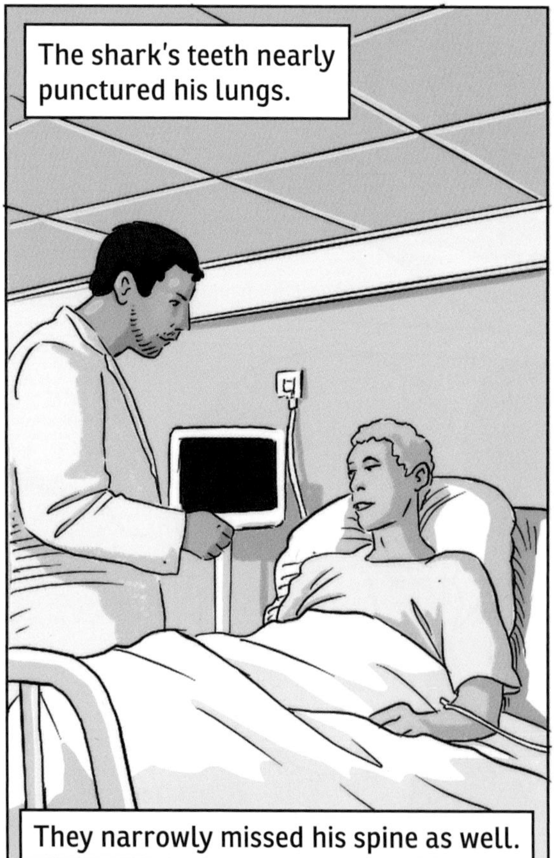
The shark's teeth nearly punctured his lungs.
They narrowly missed his spine as well.

He had lost half of the blood in his body—but he had survived!

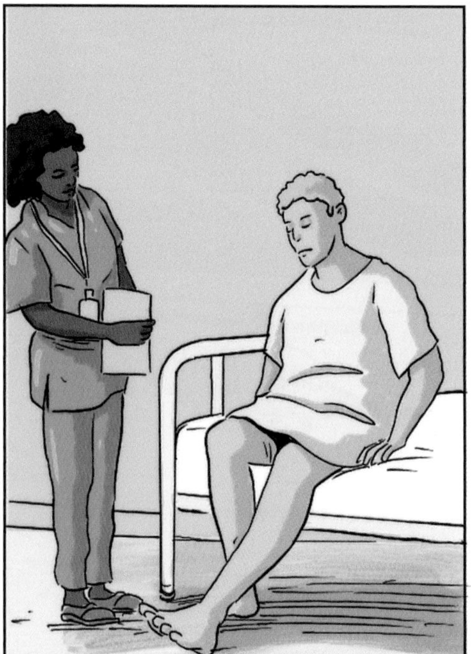

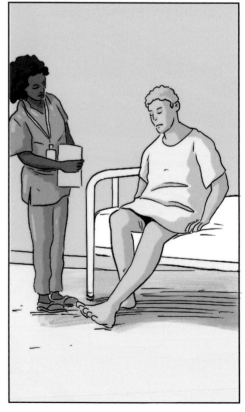

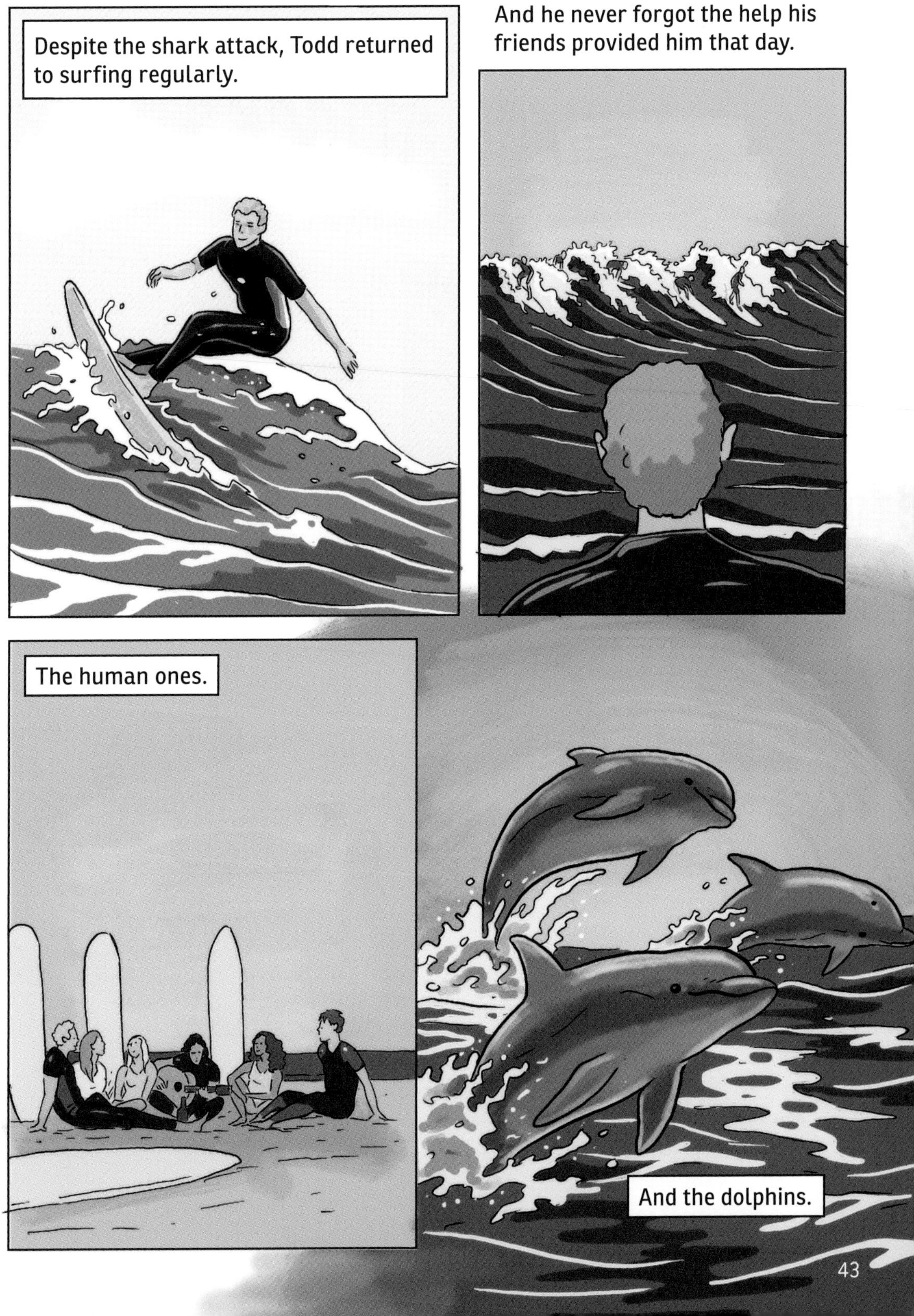
Despite the shark attack, Todd returned to surfing regularly.
And he never forgot the help his friends provided him that day.
The human ones.
And the dolphins.

MORE ABOUT
ANIMAL ATTACKS

How likely is a bear attack? The U.S. National Park Service says they are extremely rare. They usually only happen if the bear is startled or hungry.

How likely is a hippo attack? Also very rare! Hippos usually have no interest in humans. But they are very territorial and will protect their home waters.

How likely is a shark attack? Super rare! The chance of being attacked by a shark is about one in 3.7 million. There are only about 70 shark attacks per year worldwide.

In 2020, Todd Endris' shark attack was retold during the *Discovery Channel*'s famous *Shark Week*. It appeared in an episode of *I Was Prey: Terrors From the Deep*.

The best way to avoid animal attacks is simple: let wild animals be wild. Don't get near them, don't try to pet them, and only watch them from a safe distance.

GLOSSARY

femur (FEE-muhr)—the bone that extends from the pelvis to the knee

pod (POD)—a group of dolphins

predator (PRED-uh-tur)—an animal that hunts other animals for food

prey (PRAY)—an animal that is hunted by another animal for food

puncture (PUHNGK-chur)—a hole made by a sharp object

route (ROUT)—the road or course followed to get somewhere

spine (SPINE)—the backbone of a person or animal

staple (STAY-puhl)—a metal fastener used to hold layers of skin together to close a wound

stitches (STICH-es)—thread used to hold layers of skin together to close a wound

territorial (terr-uh-TOR-ee-uhl)—protective of one's area

INTERNET SITES

National Geographic Kids: 10 Hippo Facts!
natgeokids.com/uk/discover/animals/general-animals/ten-hippo-facts

National Park Service: Staying Safe Around Bears
nps.gov/subjects/bears/safety.htm

NOAA Fisheries: 12 Shark Facts that May Surprise You
fisheries.noaa.gov/feature-story/12-shark-facts-may-surprise-you

BOOKS IN THE SERIES

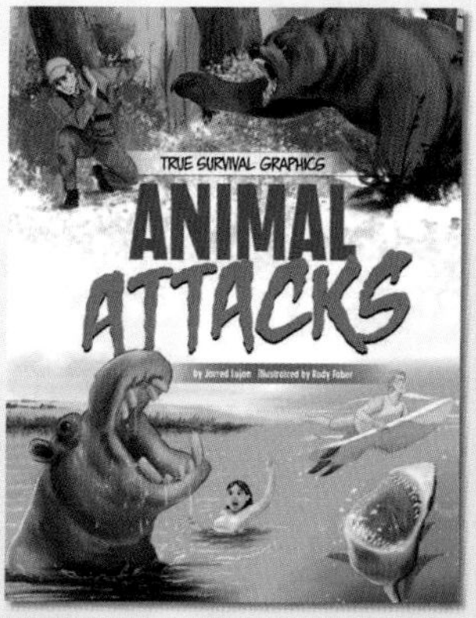
TRUE SURVIVAL GRAPHICS
ANIMAL ATTACKS

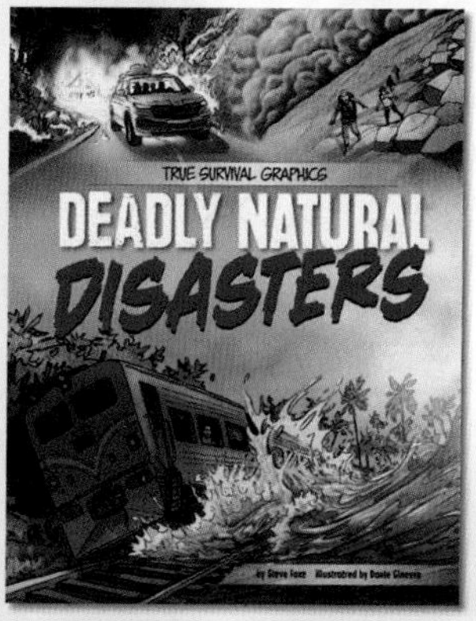
TRUE SURVIVAL GRAPHICS
DEADLY NATURAL DISASTERS

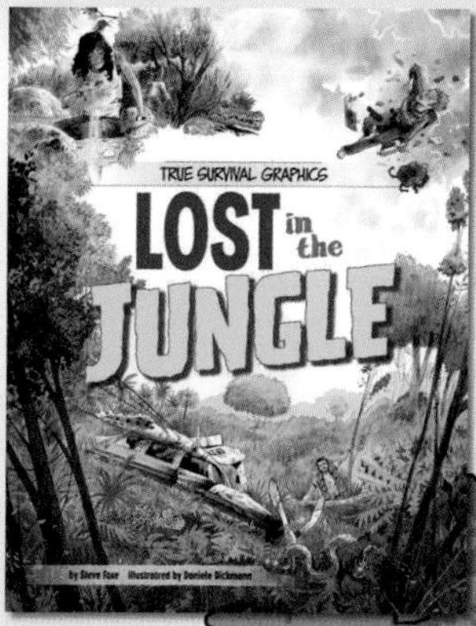
TRUE SURVIVAL GRAPHICS
LOST in the JUNGLE

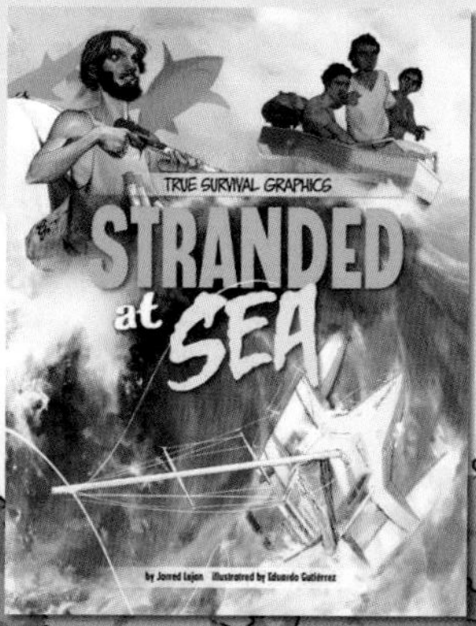
TRUE SURVIVAL GRAPHICS
STRANDED at SEA

ABOUT THE AUTHOR

Photo by Jarred Luján

Jarred Luján is a Mexican-American comic writer from the borderlands of Texas. He's a 2019 Mad Cave Studios Talent Search winner and a member of the inaugural 2022 DC Milestone Initiative class. Aside from writing, Jarred spends his time trying to convince his cats to be nice to him (his dog remains as loyal as ever).

ABOUT THE ILLUSTRATOR

Photo by Rudy Faber

Rudy Faber is a Dutch illustrator living and working in the beautiful city of Leeuwarden, Netherlands. He has worked two years as a full-time concept artist for an indie game developer and has worked on various other game projects as a freelancer. Rudy then went on to work as an illustrator mainly on books for young readers. He likes those projects the best. Apart from drawing and painting, Rudy loves to build with Lego and ride his mountain bike.